PSALMS

REAL HELP FOR REAL LIFE

RAY ORTLUND

Lifeway Press®
Brentwood, Tennessee

EDITORIAL TEAM

Cynthia Hopkins
Writer

Reid Patton
Senior Editor

Angel Prohaska
Associate Editor

Jon Rodda
Art Director

Tyler Quillet
Managing Editor

Joel Polk
Publisher, Small Group Publishing

Brian Daniel
Director, Adult Ministry Publishing

Published by Lifeway Press® • © 2023 Ray Ortlund

ISBN 978-1-0877-7825-9 • Item 005840905

Dewey decimal classification: 223.2
Subject headings: BIBLE. O.T. PSALMS \ GOD \ MEDITATION

To order additional copies of this resource, write to Lifeway Resources Customer Service; 200 Powell Place, Suite 100; Brentwood, TN 37027-7707; fax 615-251-5933; call toll free 800-458-2772; order online at lifeway.com; email orderentry@lifeway.com.

Printed in the United States of America

Adult Ministry Publishing • Lifeway Resources
200 Powell Place, Suite 100 • Brentwood, TN 37027-7707

CONTENTS

ABOUT THE AUTHOR

Ray Ortlund received a BA from Wheaton College; a ThM from Dallas Theological Seminary; an MA from the University of California, Berkeley; and a PhD from the University of Aberdeen, Scotland. Pastor Ortlund served as associate professor of Old Testament and semitic languages at Trinity Evangelical Divinity School in Deerfield, Illinois, from 1989–1998.

He was ordained by Lake Avenue Congregational Church in Pasadena, California in 1975. He served as the pastor of Immanuel Church in Nashville, Tennessee (an Acts 29 church), is a council member with the Gospel Coalition, and is the president of Renewal Ministries. Ray has been married to Jani Giles Ortlund for fifty happy years, and they have fifteen delightful grandchildren.

HOW TO USE THIS STUDY

This Bible study provides a guided process for individuals and small groups to know and understand the Psalms. Six sessions of study examine the Psalms through six key felt needs. Through the study we will meet the God who meets us where we are and offers real help for real life.

GROUP STUDY

Regardless of what day of the week your group meets, each session of content begins with the group session. Each group session uses the following format to facilitate simple yet meaningful interaction among group members and with God's Word.

START

The group session will begin with a few questions designed to help you introduce the session's topic of study and encourage everyone to engage with the study.

WATCH

Beyond Ray's teaching outline, this page is intentionally left blank for you to take notes during the group teaching. Codes to access the teaching videos are included with your purchase of this book and can be found on the insert located at the back of this book.

DISCUSS

This section is the main component of the group session. The questions provided are designed to facilitate the group study of the session's topic. The goal is to better understand God's heart and how the Psalms offer us real and immediate help in a variety of circumstances.

PERSONAL STUDY

Three days of personal study are provided after each group session to help individuals think biblically about the session's topic. With biblical teaching and introspective questions, these lessons challenge individuals to grow in their understanding of God's Word and to respond in faith and obedience.

PERSONAL BIBLE STUDY 1 AND 2

The group and personal studies are complimentary. The first personal Bible study takes a fuller look at the psalm being studied in the group and expands on the content and themes from the group teaching. The second personal Bible study examines another psalm with a similar theme. These studies are meant to deepen your understanding of the Psalms and give you more concentrated time to reflect upon and apply what you learned in the group session. The personal study section ends with a journaling activity designed to help members distill key truths.

GOING DEEPER

In addition to the group video teaching, this study includes one personal study video per session where Ray helps you become a better reader of the Psalms. These videos can be accessed by redeeming the access code found on the insert in the back of this book.

LEADER GUIDE

A cutout leader guide for each session is provided on pages 128–42, which highlights key points from each session and offers helpful considerations for leading a group discussion. Additionally, you'll find tips for helping you lead a small group.

REAL HELP FOR REAL LIFE

GROUP STUDY

START

Welcome everyone to session 1, "Real Help for Real Life."

Ask participants to introduce themselves. As they do, invite them to find and share one verse from the Psalms that's meaningful to them. This can be a favorite verse or a verse they find in the moment.

What are some emotions we might experience reading and studying the Psalms together?

John Calvin called the Psalms "an anatomy of all the parts of the soul." He explained, "There is not an emotion of which anyone can be conscious that is not here represented as in a mirror. . . . There is no other book in which is recorded so many deliverances, nor one in which the evidences and experiences of the fatherly providence and solicitude which God exercises towards us are celebrated."[1]

With this in mind, what real help for real life do you hope to gain in our study of the Psalms?

In all circumstances—joyful and tragic, confident and fearful, calm and anxious, righteous and sinful, hopeful and despairing—David and other psalmists wrote songs of prayer to God. These are not tidy, polite, or fake. They are the honest expressions from real people getting real with God—and finding real help. As such, they teach us what it's like to encounter the living God. They help us answer the questions: Who is God really? Who am I really? And what happens when those two collide?

We'll begin our study in Psalms 1 and 2, as a way of discovering the direction of the entire book. As we begin the first video session, let's invite God to speak to us.

> *Father, we need to rediscover and experience You as personal, vivid, and real each and every day. Give us new insight into Your heart as it is connected into our mess. We want to know You—not hypothetically or only as doctrine, but as our moment by moment presence and help in every need.*

---

1. John Calvin, *Commentary on the Book of Psalms*, translated by James Anderson (Grand Rapids: Eerdmans, 1949), xxxvii–xxxviii.

WATCH

Use these statements to follow along as you watch video session 1.

Three things to notice in Psalms 1 and 2:

1. These two psalms introduce the whole book.

2. Psalm 1 is marked with strong contrasts, with wise personal guidance.

3. Psalm 2 is equally bold, with hope for the entire world.

To access the teaching sessions,
use the instructions in the back
of your Bible study book.

DISCUSS

Use these questions and prompts to discuss the video teaching.

Read Psalms 1 and 2. In your view, what statement of truth do these two psalms together make?

Ray gave three insights to help us get the most out of Psalms 1 and 2.

1. These two psalms introduce the whole book.

Who is blessed in Psalm 1:1? In what way?

Who is blessed in Psalm 2:12? In what way? How are the blessings of these verses related?

Do you most often pray and relate to God in a personal or worldwide context? Why? Why are both necessary?

Is it possible to truly experience personal renewal apart from confidence in worldwide renewal, or vice versa? Explain.

2. Psalm 1 is marked with strong contrasts, with wise personal guidance.

What does the pattern of "Not this, but that" in Psalm 1 make boldly clear?

We asked God to show Himself to us not hypothetically but as personal, vivid, and real each and every moment. And in the video teaching, Ray explained, "Psalm 1 is a flag-planting psalm that helps us be decisive." So let's personalize it.

What should Psalm 1 help you be decisive about? What clear contrast does your life need to begin to exemplify?

3. Psalm 2 is equally bold, with hope for the entire world..

How would you describe the overall message and tone of Psalm 2?

What does it mean to take refuge in the Lord?

Our world, like the world of David, the world of the first Christians (Acts 4:23-31), and the world of every generation, is filled with people in angry internal and external war, refusing to take refuge in the Lord. At the very same time, Jesus offers the hope of eternal blessing to all who turn to Him.

In what situation do you need to acknowledge the evil around you and pray for boldness to speak and act with the certain hope of Christ?

What remaining questions or comments do you have about this session's teaching video? What was challenging, convicting, encouraging, or timely for your current circumstances?

CLOSE IN PRAYER

Prayer Requests

_____

_____

_____

PSALM 1

OUTLINE OF PSALM 1

The Present: The believer flourishes, the wicked decline (1-4)
The Future: The Lord will preserve the righteous, and them only (5-6)

Psalms is a book of sacred songs—songs of praise and songs of lament. In fact, the Psalter (the book of the psalms) was the hymnbook of the temple; its content filled Israel's personal and corporate worship. It is interesting, then, that Psalm 1, which stands as the introduction to the biblical hymnbook, focuses on "the law of the LORD."

Read Psalm 1.

Why would "the law of the LORD" stand out as the emphasis of the very first song in the Psalter? What does this teach you about worship?

We step into the worship of God through and according to the Word of God. It's not as though we're worshiping God when we're singing, and then the sermon is something else. Christians worship God by singing the Bible, praying the Bible, reading the Bible, preaching the Bible, and hearing the Bible. Psalm 1 puts the gospel at the forefront of biblical worship, because *the biblical message alone* can lift us to God in worship that is pleasing to Him. Worship is the human response to the presence of the Lord. And since the Lord is ever present, worship is a whole-life practice.

What principles in Psalm 1 can you apply to your personal worship?

Psalm 1 instructs our heads and woos our hearts, because God wants to free us from disorder and distraction within to worship Him with both our head and heart.

TRUTH FOR OUR HEADS

Psalm 1 offers God's truth for our heads as the first step away from false worship and into the true worship of God. It replaces our idolatry—"the counsel of the wicked"—with the law of the Lord as the only finally convincing and fruitful object of the mind's meditation. The word *meditates* in Psalm 1:2 is neither a dreamy religious laziness nor an uninvolved intellectual sport, but a profoundly personal internalizing of biblical truth. Meditation is human thought at its best, and it is essential to true worship.

Read the following verses and identify the truths God wants you to affirm and confess:

> **Psalm 14:1**

> **Psalm 92:5**

> **Psalm 145:3-5**

Which of these truths stand out to you most personally right now as real help for real life? Why?

Psalm 1 defines two ways of life and the choices related to them with no ambiguities. The word *not* appears six times in six verses in the original text, and the word *but* appears three times. The logic of the psalm is clear: "Not this, but that."

Describe what Psalm 1 teaches regarding "not this, but that":

> (Verses 1-2) Not _____,

> but _____.

> (Verses 3-4) Not _____,

> but _____.

> (Verses 5-6) Not _____,

> but _____.

TRUTH FOR OUR HEARTS

God has defined our choices clearly, yet we struggle between them. The problem is that even when our heads possess knowledge, our hearts can be divided. We sometimes want it both ways. Because of this, we form our thoughts on issues like sexuality, money, success, and numerous other things based on our preferences rather than God's Word.

Because God loves sinners whose hearts are divided, He does not simply leave us with an intellectual choice. He provides the breakthrough our hearts desperately need. In Psalm 1 God invites us to trade in our preferences for His love in Christ as the defining center of everything we are. Being a Christian means that we now define ourselves in relation to Christ. Christ, not self, defines a life worth living.

Read Romans 12:1-2. In what situation(s) are you tempted to conform to the counsel of the sinful world? Why?

God calls you to be transformed, or redefined, by the renewing of your mind. Consider Psalm 1 and Romans 12:1-2 together. How does our renewal take place?

Psalm 1:1 begins with the word *blessed* **to describe the one who worships God rightly with both head and heart. From verses 3-6, what does it mean to be blessed?**

The word *blessed* is a congratulatory formula. In other words, in Psalm 1:1, God is saying to those who have become decisive in taking a stand for Christ, "Way to go!" Through Christ, God is willing to be the head cheerleader of everyone who worships Him according to His Word. Beyond cheering us on, God enriches our worship as He enables us to grow, bear fruit, not wither, and prosper in a way that will satisfy our hearts forever.

In what situation do you need to become decisive in taking a stand for Christ? Why is it important that you do?

What does Psalm 1 say about the idea that you can be a "casual Christian"?

The word *delight* in Psalm 1:2 raises the bar for worship by reminding us that there is no such thing as half-hearted, play-it-safe, keep-a-low-profile Christianity. The Christian faith is gladly wholehearted. Given who God is, "the law of the LORD" cannot be a wearying imposition. It can be the object of our highest delight. But the word *delight* also lowers the bar. You don't need a PhD to be refreshed by the Bible. You only need love for Christ.

Read John 5:39. What should we be looking for as we read and memorize and meditate on the Bible?

TRUTH FROM CHRIST

The Bible isn't a set of principles for living the Christian life. The Bible is the story of God not abandoning us but coming down to us through Christ, though it cost Him His life. And seeing Jesus as the key to everything in the Bible makes the whole Book come alive. If we read the Bible as the endless display of Christ in His many glories, "the law of the LORD" will never stop activating our worship.

Does Psalm 1:3 mean that those who delight in God's Word will always have an easy and comfortable life? How do you know?

Read Psalm 73:2-3 and 17. We experience times of weakness in which our deep enjoyment of God's Word will falter. Does this mean that the promises in Psalm 1:3 are not ours during hardship? What does it mean?

Reread Psalm 1:5-6.

The word *therefore* is the hinge on which Psalm 1 turns from time to eternity. Verses 1-4 are in the present tense. Then verse 5 fast-forwards into the future, all the way into the eternal state. Verses 1-4 are about how we live now; verse 5 describes eternity as we shall experience it then.

Psalm 1 is clear: *Delight determines destiny.* How should this truth impact daily life?

In terms of the struggles of daily life, what does it mean to you that "the LORD knows the way of the righteous" (v. 6)?

If you want to worship Christ but sometimes you feel unable, the Lord knows you. He understands you. He is involved with you. He has chosen you for Himself, He has inclined you toward Himself, He is calling you to Himself, and His grace will hold onto you forever. Rest in that today.

PSALM 1
REAL HELP FOR REAL LIFE

Use the spaces below to journal a prayer or response to each prompt.

COUNSEL. Do you wonder what is the best way to live? You don't have to! God clearly shows you in His Word what is righteous and wicked.

CLARITY. There is only one way to turn from idolatry to worship—reject your own formulas for blessedness, and let God redefine you with the blessedness of Christ.

CONTENTMENT. The righteous of Psalm 1 are idolatrous sinners whose sin was nailed to Christ on the cross. God offers Jesus's righteousness as your new standing in His presence.

CONFIDENCE. If you are in Christ, your future is hopeful and bright—ready for Psalm 2, Psalm 3, Psalm 4—all the way through the Psalter, to the great hallelujahs of Psalms 146–150 in that perfect temple above.

CONSTANCY. If you want to worship God, shut the distractions out and pick up your Bible. Open it, read it, believe it, meditate on it, delight in it, obey it. God will show you Christ. He will refresh you and help you, from now on into eternity.

PSALM 2

OUTLINE OF PSALM 2

The psalmist asks: Why do the nations rage? (1-3)
God responds: The Lord laughs (4-6)
The Messiah declares: This world is His (7-9)
The psalmist advises: Surrender to the true King (10-12)

As the gateway into the Psalter, Psalms 1 and 2 zoom in and out. Psalm 1 zooms in to emphasize our individual reality with the living God. Then Psalm 2 zooms out to show us the macro reality—our Messiah is a conquering King, having absolute rule over the entire world. Both psalms help us discover God—not hypothetically, but as personal and present, moment by moment.

Read Psalm 2:1-12.

List the words and phrases about God that stand out to you, along with any questions, concerns, or feelings those descriptors raise.

Psalm 2 could be described as the ancient Israelite national anthem. It celebrates the struggle between the kingdom of God and the kingdom of man, with God's victory through Messiah.

The psalmist took his stand in this conflict. He was devoted to God. He was astonished to see the nations of the world conspiring to overthrow God's kingdom. With a sense of outrage he picked up his pen to alert us to what is happening in the world, to assure us of God's victory, and to call us to commitment.

This psalm consists of four paragraphs of three verses each. In the first paragraph, the psalmist points to world events, turns to us, and asks a question.

OUR QUESTION

Reread Psalm 2:1-3. What point is the psalmist making with this opening question?

Where do you see evidence of the world raging against God today?

Everywhere we look we see people trying to construct an alternative reality that excludes the authority of God. The important thing to grasp is that people move in crazy directions because they are rebelling against *God*. That is what the psalmist is helping us to see in verse 1. There is no peace in this world because the world resents divine authority.

What does verse 3 indicate about how the world perceives the rule of God?

Read Matthew 28:18-20. What connection is there between Jesus's words to us here and Psalm 2:1-3?

All around us there is a rebellious attempt to build a world without God. This is why the church is so important. It is a constant reminder that God is still there, and that life under God is freedom and blessing, not chains and slavery.

How has the community of faith pointed you back to God at the time when you needed it most?

GOD'S LAUGHTER

In the second paragraph, we find out how God feels about what is happening.

> **Reread Psalm 2:4-6. Does God's laughter mean He is insensitive to the effects of rebellion in the world or that He thinks it's funny? What does God's laughter teach us about Him?**

As God looks down at this world, He is not biting His nails with sweat running down His face. He is totally unthreatened. He views human rebellion—however powerful and sophisticated—with contempt. In comparison to His power and authority, the attempts of rebellious people to throw off that authority is laughable. No one can knock God off His throne.

We know that God is gracious toward all His creatures. But He doesn't worry. He is in control, enthroned above in the heavens, and will conclude the day of grace when He wishes.

> **How does recognizing God's sovereign control change your perspective on world events?**

> **What about your own personal struggles?**

In the first four verses, the psalmist looked out at the world scene. In verses 5-6, he looked forward into the future, when God will step in decisively to put a stop to the world's conspiracy.

> **Read 1 Thessalonians 5:2-3. What do these verses teach us about the forms of "peace and security" we construct that exclude God's authority?**

In the third paragraph, the Messiah speaks.

Reread Psalm 2:7-9 to see Jesus and His authority.

Read Acts 13:32-33. What is the "today" referred to in Psalm 2:7?

This psalm is a declaration of the messianic office, which many Israelite kings occupied but which only Jesus fulfills. In Acts 13 Paul quoted Psalm 2 to explain that our Lord's resurrection and ascension into glory were His coronation as King of the world. God has fulfilled His promise through the resurrection of Christ.

Read Colossians 1:16-17. Why is it important to believe that "begotten" is different from "created"?

Read Hebrews 1:1-5. What does God's declaration of sonship teach us about Jesus's kingship and authority?

Read John 5:22. What does it mean that God has given Jesus the nations and ends of the earth as His heritage and possession (Psalm 2:8)?

Christ is not the son of God in the sense that He is "God Jr." Rather, the Son shares the Father's divine being and essence. As the Nicene Creed says, Christ is "begotten not made." He is God's anointed, eternal King with absolute authority over this world. In comparison, even the most powerful among us are like clay pots that He can shatter to pieces. God is not saying to us, "Here is Christ. Take Him or leave Him." God is saying, "Here is Christ. Take Him, accept Him *as your king.*"

A CLOSING ADMONITION

The poet concludes with some advice for us all.

Reread Psalm 2:10-12. What did the psalmist say the kings of the earth should do?

How does that apply to you?

What changes would take place in your life this week if you were to truly take refuge in Christ?

God sent Christ to offer peace to anyone who is willing to come under His authority. That's true for all of us, whether we hold great power or little. The call is to voluntarily accept the authority of Jesus as rightful King of the universe. When we do, we take refuge in the One who truly possesses all authority.

Psalm 2, then, zooms out to widen our view of the reality made clear in Psalm 1—there are only two options. We can either take refuge in the one true King, or we can suffer the wrath of the one true King. There is refuge *in* Christ from the wrath to come, open to all who seek Him in faith, but there is no refuge *from* Christ.

Why is this message of Jesus's royal ultimacy *good* news for us?

PSALM 2

REAL HELP FOR REAL LIFE

Use the spaces below to journal a prayer or response to each prompt.

RESOLVE. There was a radical edge to the psalmist's faith. He expressed a sense of outrage regarding human rebellion against the Lord. He refused to accept the charade of human autonomy. What about you? Jesus is King. Does He have your full allegiance, loyalty, purpose, and passion in life?

STRENGTH. The Lord reigns—unafraid, steady, resolute, sovereign—over everyone and everything and He is *for you*. What opposition causes you to feel weak? The reality is that in Christ, human opposition counts for nothing.

JOY. The introduction to the Psalter begins with "blessed" (1:1) and then comes back around to end with the same word (2:12). "Blessed are all who take refuge in him," then, isn't simply a throwaway thought. The blessing for righteous worshipers of King Jesus is uninhibited joy forever. Your everlasting future is described further in Isaiah 35:10. Describe that scene in your own words.

HOW TO READ THE PSALMS

In the Going Deeper teaching, Ray gives three helps for reading and understanding the Psalms:

1. POETIC STRUCTURE—parallel lines working together to build and enhance understanding.

2. IMAGERY—opening our eyes to dimensions of God's care and commitment that might never have occurred to us.

3. TYPES—psalms of praise and psalms of lament, joy, and pain, with patterns emerging in both.

As a way of putting these helps into practice, take a look again at Psalms 1 and 2. Examine and consider these two psalms in light of the three helps according to the prompts below.

POETRY. List any parallel lines in Psalms 1 and 2 that serve to build and enhance understanding for you. Specifically, how do these lines enrich your understanding of the psalm's meaning?

IMAGERY. Identify any imagery in Psalms 1 and 2 that makes the truth more vivid and real to you. What clarity do these figures of speech give you about the reality of who God is, who you are, or what happens when those two collide?

TYPES. Choose from the list below what types of psalms are Psalms 1 and 2 (there can be more than one).

WISDOM—instructive psalms that provide practical guidelines for godly living.

MESSIANIC—royal psalms that portray Christ as the undisputed sovereign King.

LAMENT—impassioned psalms that cry out to God for deliverance from trouble.

IMPRECATORY—provocative psalms that invoke God's wrath and judgment on enemies.

THANKSGIVING—grateful psalms that express a profound awareness of God's blessings.

PILGRIMAGE— festive psalms that promote a celebrative mood of praise as Israel, while traveling to Jerusalem for the annual feasts, recollect God's goodness to them.

ENTHRONEMENT—awe-inspiring psalms that describe the majesty and providential care of God's sovereign rule.

Now note the emergent pattern or flow of thought in Psalm 1. Psalm 2 is given as an example.

Psalm 1:

Psalm 2:
Humanity's rebellion against God (vv. 1-3), God's response to rebellion (vv. 4-6), the Messiah's divine authority (vv. 7-9), resulting instruction for humanity (vv. 10-12).

To access the teaching sessions, use the instructions in the back of your Bible study book.

REAL REST

GROUP STUDY

START

Welcome the group to session 2, "Real Rest."
Before introducing session 2, take a few minutes to review session 1.

Before starting the new content each week, we'll spend some time talking about insights we discovered during the previous week's personal study. The review questions will be simple, designed to help us press into the real help for real life God gives us in the Psalms.

What real-life issues did your study of Psalms 1 and 2 address for you?

What real help did Psalms 1 and 2 offer you?

Which of the three insights for studying the Psalms in Going Deeper stood out to you as particularly helpful? How so?

Throughout the Psalms, we find the psalmists wrestling with significant difficulties and traumatic events. Where they might be prone to fearful panic, we find them instead demonstrating full trust and confidence in the Lord. This week, we're going to come alongside them to find the reason for their trust and confidence—God's ever-present provision through real calm and rest in a world of chaos.

In what current situation do you need God's help of real rest?

To prepare for video session 2, pray that God will help
each person understand and apply this truth:

> You never have to face life and the challenges
> before you as if all you have going for you is you.

WATCH

Use these statements to follow along as you watch video session 2.

To make the most of Psalm 23, consider these three aspects:

1. The personal nature of the psalm.

2. The trajectory of the psalm.

3. The spirit of the psalm.

To access the teaching sessions,
use the instructions in the back
of your Bible study book.

DISCUSS

Use these questions and prompts to discuss the video teaching.

Read Psalm 23. Why do you think this psalm is so well-known and loved? In the past, how has Psalm 23 been meaningful to you?

To make the most of Psalm 23, Ray suggested that we consider these three aspects:

1. The personal nature of the psalm.

2. The trajectory of the psalm.

3. The spirit of the psalm.

Why is finding real rest for the soul a personal, individual matter?

Ray explained that there will be a time when we will each face a crisis alone. This side of that crisis, how can you know if your faith is your own or if you're depending on someone else's faith?

Consider the assurances that David expresses in Psalm 23. Which of these do you share? Which of his declarations do you struggle to make your own? Why?

David faced moments of crisis, too. Those crises did not define his life. Instead, he experienced great success because he grew to know the Lord personally—as shepherd, host, and God. In light of the reality of who God is, David also grew to understand himself as a sheep, a guest, and a worshiper. Whatever the stage of life or circumstances he faced, David's story was always getting better—and so is ours.

How do you tend to think about the trajectory of your life—as being on the rise or in decline? Why?

How does verse 6 encourage you in your present circumstance?

What additional insights do the following New Testament verses teach you about the trajectory of life David asserts in Psalm 23:6?

    Romans 8:28-29—

    Philippians 2:13—

    Hebrews 12:7-11—

Even when we have confidence that we will "dwell in the house of the LORD forever" it can be difficult to believe that goodness and mercy will follow us all the days of our earthly lives. But God is always at work for His glory and our ultimate good. This is why Psalm 23 reflects such calm assurance.

Ray used the words *rest, calmness,* and *expectancy* to describe the spirit of Psalm 23. Which of these words stands out to you personally as especially instructive about your relationship with the Lord? Explain.

What situation tempts you to think, speak, or act as if all you have going for you is you? How does Psalm 23 encourage you in that situation?

What remaining questions or comments do you have about this session's teaching video? What was challenging, convicting, encouraging, or timely for your current circumstances?

CLOSE IN PRAYER

Prayer Requests

PSALM 23

OUTLINE OF PSALM 23
The Lord as Shepherd (1-4)
The Lord as Host (5)
The Lord as God (6)

Community matters so much, but the time is coming when you will face *the* crisis of your life all by yourself—in some way, shape, or form. You will need Jesus. That event will make clear that you need Jesus every moment of every day. Psalm 23 faithfully guides us to the rest that Jesus provides.

Read Psalm 23. Note the personal pronouns used throughout. What do these instances teach us about God's personal care for each of us?

When have you experienced the personal nature of the rest God provides?

In what situation do you need to experience God's rest personally now?

While the Christian faith includes the glorious grace of helpful community, the heart of the psalm is David saying (and us saying along with him), "The LORD is *my* shepherd." We see no community in Psalm 23. When David first sang this song, he sang it alone.

The personal, individual focus of this psalm is not selfish. Real rest for your heart, mind, and soul can come no other way than to actively trust in Jesus and never stop. To better understand the personal nature of the rest God provides, consider the truths presented in Psalm 23.

TRUTH ACCORDING TO PSALM 23

The LORD is my shepherd; I shall not want.

PSALM 23:1

Which of the following statements best reflects the meaning of Psalm 23:1?

☐ Don't worry. Be happy!

☐ Whatever will be, will be, and I should be fine with it.

☐ God is in charge; I shouldn't want any of my circumstances to change.

☐ Because of who Jesus is to me—responsible, committed, attentive, caring, and always involved—I am content.

"The LORD is my shepherd" stands as the heading over all of verses 1-4. Then the rest of these verses tell us more about what it means and what it's worth that the Lord is your Shepherd. Life is hard. You are busy. But life in Christ is rest in motion. You can know that, whatever happens, you will be okay because Jesus Himself has made sure of it. The whole Bible keeps helping us get into this calm frame of mind.

From the following verses, what reasons do you have to be content?

Genesis 15:1

John 1:16

Revelation 22:17

God is not stingy or small. Christ has more than enough blessing for all our needs forever, and Psalm 23 is saying to you personally, you can have Him—all of Him—for your needs. He's not holding back. Why would you?

How are you sometimes tempted to fill in the blank below?

The Lord plus _____
are my shepherds.

What is the danger of trying to follow multiple shepherds?

JESUS + NOTHING = EVERYTHING

We struggle to rest when our hearts start saying, "The Lord plus _____ are my shepherds." What we're *really* saying is that _____ is my shepherd. But the only true Shepherd is the risen Jesus. The way to find real rest is to let go of every false shepherd, and take Jesus in all His fullness.

> You prepare a table before me
> > in the presence of my enemies;
> you anoint my head with oil;
> > my cup overflows.
>
> **PSALM 23:5**

The second metaphor used in Psalm 23 portrays the Lord as your Host. What does God provide as your "Host"?

What is the relationship between God's provision and rest for your heart, mind, and soul?

When have you experienced the Lord's provision and rest in your need?

...ho do not trust Jesus as Shepherd ...st in Him as a rebuke. But when ...o amount of opposition can block ...enemy is, if Jesus is your friend? ...r journey in ways you can't explain.

...y shall follow me

...se of the LORD

The metaphors disappear, and we enter into literal reality. The "house of the LORD" is God's temple, the place of His felt presence. To be the Lord's sheep is good. To be the Lord's guest is better. But to be caught up in His glory? The word for that is *heaven*. No shadow of death, no evil, no enemies—the Lord Himself will be your joy forever.

Read Romans 8:38-39. How does Paul express the message of Psalm 23:6?

Read Philippians 1:6. What rest is there for your soul in those times when your heart does wander off?

God's goodness and mercy, not His wrath and judgment, will keep pursuing you. That's what the verb translated "follow" in verse 6 actually means. The Lord isn't catching up to us; He is chasing us down. God doesn't wait for His worshipers to come to Him; He goes out and finds us and brings us in. And then He brings us back in, many times, until there is no shadow of death, no threat of enemies, nor even the impulse in our own hearts to wander off. We are perfectly at rest in Him.

PSALM 23
REAL REST

Here is the great thing about Jesus our Shepherd, our Host, our God: He can outrun us any day of the week. And He will—faithfully. Our problem of heart, mind, and soul rest isn't about who Jesus is; it's about our rejection of the reality of who He is. When we do not follow Him as Shepherd, receive His provision as Host, and worship Him as God, our perspective on reality gets wrapped up in an exhausting lie. We will still face those crises of life all by ourselves, needing Jesus personally. Yet, in those moments, our singular pronouns will offer no hope—only despair.

Consider David Powlison's Antipsalm 23:

> I'm on my own.
> No one looks out for me or protects me.
> I experience a continual sense of need.
> Nothing's quite right.
> I'm always restless.
> I'm easily frustrated and often disappointed.
> It's a jungle—I feel overwhelmed.
> It's a desert—I'm thirsty.
> My soul feels broken, twisted, and stuck.
> I can't fix myself.
> I stumble down some dark paths.
> Still, I insist: I want to do what I want, when I want, how I want.
> But life's confusing.
> Why don't things ever really work out?
> I'm haunted by emptiness and futility—shadows of death.
> I fear the big hurt and final loss.
> Death is waiting for me at the end of every road,
> but I'd rather not think about that.
> I spend my life protecting myself.
> Bad things can happen.
> I find no lasting comfort.
> I'm alone . . . facing everything that could hurt me.
> Are my friends really friends?
> Other people use me for their own ends.
> I can't really trust anyone.

No one has my back.
No one is really for me—except me.
And I'm so much all about ME, sometimes it's sickening.
I belong to no one except myself.
My cup is never quite full enough.
I'm left empty.
Disappointment follows me all the days of my life.
Will I just be obliterated into nothingness?
Will I be alone forever, homeless, free-falling into void?
Sartre said, "Hell is other people."
I have to add, "Hell is also myself."
It's a living death,
    and then I die.[1]

Underline any statements in the antipsalm that you are prone to believe.

Now read Psalm 23 again. What statements of reality contradict those thoughts you underlined?

Write those truths beside the statements you marked.

1. David Powlison, "Sane Faith in the Insanity of Life (Part 1)," Christian Counseling & Educational Foundation, May 19, 2009, www.ccef.org/sane-faith-insanity-life/.

PSALM 130

OUTLINE FOR PSALM 130

Real faith cries out to God (1-2)
Real grace humbles us to revere the Lord (3-4)
Real faith yearns for God (5-6)
Real grace lavishly redeems all our sins (7-8)

What we're discovering is that the Psalms guide us into our personal reality with the living God. That reality is not tidy or polite, and it cannot be faked. What matters most about you is how you see God. Without a right vision of God, there is no right understanding of self—and no real rest.

Read Psalm 130.
Which of the following best characterizes the psalmist's need?

help in an outward circumstance

rescue from enemies

rescue from the sin within

help overcoming temptation

Can you relate to the psalmist's emotion regarding his need, or does it seem strange to you? Why?

What is the relationship between repentance and rest?

Psalm 130 is a psalm of sorrowful lament, teaching us that a person of real faith is honest about their struggles. But real faith doesn't stagnate in struggle; it breaks through to hope, overflowing confidence, and plentiful redemption. And where there is redemption, there is real rest.

STRUGGLING IN HONESTY

> Out of the depths I cry to you, O LORD!
>   O Lord, hear my voice!
> Let your ears be attentive
>   to the voice of my pleas for mercy!
> **PSALM 130:1-2**

How would you characterize the psalmist's state of mind?

What are some different ways people respond when they feel distant from God or a sense of God's disapproval?

What does Psalm 130:1-2 teach you about the way back to God?

The psalmist had sunk down to a place of profoundly felt distance from God, overwhelmed with a sense of God's disapproval and disfavor. He knew that he had sinned deeply and that God forgives sin (v. 4), but he did not yet have a felt sense of God's deep forgiveness. In fact, he felt forsaken by God. And that is a deep pit. But Psalm 130 also points the way back to God—urgent honesty with God that forsakes appearances and cries out in humility.

Read Mark 2:17. To whom does Jesus give rest?

Through the finished work of Christ on the cross, and in Christ alone, we experience forgiveness and God gives Himself to us afresh.

> If you, O LORD, should mark iniquities,
>
> O Lord, who could stand?
>
> But with you there is forgiveness,
>
> that you may be feared.
>
> **PSALM 130:3-4**

Rewrite the psalmist's "If" question in your own words.

What did the psalmist know about God?

Christianity is a religion of moral punishment and the settling of scores, but not in the way people often think. God settled the score through Jesus, who took our place as our substitute on His cross. God did enforce justice to settle the score. He demanded everything—but not of us. Christ stepped in as our willing substitute and met the demand for us. That's *why* with God there is forgiveness. He didn't sweep sin under the rug; He nailed it to the cross.

How does God want the awareness of His forgiveness to impact your life?

If we know what it means to suffer in the depths, we cannot trivialize what it cost God to lift us up. Grace does not produce reckless, arrogant people. Grace humbles us down into a different kind of depth, a sweet depth—a deep awe of the Lord: "That you may be feared" (v. 4).

I wait for the LORD, my soul waits,
    and in his word I hope;
my soul waits for the Lord
    more than watchmen for the morning,
    more than watchmen for the morning.

PSALM 130:5-6

What was the psalmist now waiting for? As he waited, where did he put his hope?

If your sins stand before you, accusing you, tormenting you, and dragging you down to the depths of shame and despair, God is able to speak a word of release to your heart. Look to Him, and wait for Him. He will come to you and speak His assurance, as sure as the dawn. Put your hope in Him and open your heart to the gospel as His word spoken *personally to you*, because it is.

The psalmist knows that what he needs, to pull out of the depths, is for God to personalize the gospel to his heart. God wants you to know not just that He forgives sins but that He forgives *your* sins. Verses 5-6 teach you to long for God to give you rest from the night of your gloom with the dawn of His assurance. God is able to pour out His love into your heart through the Holy Spirit as you believe Him, so that you enjoy the release of His authoritative forgiveness.

What assurances do the following verses give you about God's forgiveness?

Psalm 103:10-13

Malachi 4:2

1 John 1:7-9

HOPE IN THE LORD

O Israel, hope in the LORD!
 For with the LORD there is steadfast love,
  and with him is plentiful redemption.
And he will redeem Israel
 from all his iniquities.

PSALM 130:7-8

We saw the personal, individual emphasis of the Lord's rest in Psalm 23, and in the first six verses of Psalm 130. But here in verses 7-8, the relevance of rest broadens far beyond one person's struggle. This psalm of lament is also one of the psalms of ascent that would have been sung as the Israelites made their way to Jerusalem to celebrate the feasts and festivals. These truths helped them prepare their hearts as they made their way. They are here in the riches of God's Word to prepare all our hearts on the way.

What does the psalmist's testimony from the depths of despair teach other people to know with certainty about the Lord?

Reread verse 4. What does the communal aspect of verses 7-8 teach you about God's larger purpose in your forgiveness?

Does God intend for your experience of forgiveness to have purpose outside of yourself? How will that happen?

PSALM 130
REAL REST

Use the spaces below to journal a prayer or response to each prompt.

REMEDY. You don't have to be trapped in your own history, smallness, isolation, and sadness. Cry out to the Lord about your great need, and receive His *plentiful* forgiveness and righteousness.

ASSURANCE. If you are in Christ, then see yourself as you are—as fully forgiven as a sinner can be. And walk in that truth with joyful confidence.

RELATIONSHIPS. Every person you know who believes in Christ is a sinner as fully forgiven as they can be. There is no good reason for you to hang on to unforgiveness and let a grudge steal your joy.

SHARE. Every person who has not yet turned to Christ in faith will one day cry out of the depths for His mercy. So they need to find rest in Him now, before it's too late. Will you share the testimony He has given you?

AWE. No one else in the whole universe is as slow to anger and so rich in mercy as the God whom you have deeply offended. Why not dare to believe in the majesty of His forgiveness?

PSALMS FOR PERSONAL CALM

In the video session, Ray gave a practical tool for pressing into the Psalms to get into those green pastures and still waters and stay there. Try putting that tool into practice. Begin by underlining, circling, and/or highlighting words that stand out to you in the text of Psalm 23.

The LORD is my shepherd; I shall not want.
> He makes me lie down in green pastures.

He leads me beside still waters.
> He restores my soul.

He leads me in paths of righteousness
> for his name's sake.

Even though I walk through the valley of the shadow of death,
> I will fear no evil,

for you are with me;
> your rod and your staff,
> they comfort me.

You prepare a table before me
> in the presence of my enemies;

you anoint my head with oil;
> my cup overflows.

Surely goodness and mercy shall follow me
> all the days of my life,

and I shall dwell in the house of the LORD
> forever.

PSALM 23

Now, on the facing page, write your thoughts, prayers, and concerns as the Spirit gives you new insights into the text.

To access the teaching sessions, use the instructions in the back of your Bible study book.

REAL

HONESTY

GROUP STUDY

START

Welcome the group to session 3, "Real Honesty."
Before introducing session 3, take a few minutes to review session 2.

As we did last week, we want to spend some time reviewing the previous session and the personal study that followed. As we study the Psalms, we're finding the real help for real life God gives.

What real-life issues did your study of Psalms 23 and 130 address for you?

What real help in those issues did Psalms 23 and 130 offer you?

How did the practical tool for pressing into the Psalms in Going Deeper guide you into green pastures and still waters? How might that journaling practice help you maintain a spirit of real rest in the Lord?

In the chaos of this world, it's tough to rest in a spirit of calm. The Psalms, though, teach us that the Lord is deserving of our hope and confidence. A spirit of rest isn't a hypothetical musing. It shows itself real in times of external trouble, and even internal conflict when we have sinned against the Lord. This week, we're going to discover the role honesty and repentance play in finding real help for real life.

In what current situation do you need God's help of real honesty?

To prepare for video session 3, pray that God will help
each person understand and apply this truth:

Real faith asks hard questions, struggles, and faces the very things about ourselves that scare us the most.

WATCH

Use these statements to follow along as you watch video session 3.

Three insights to help get the most out of Psalm 51:

1. The backstory.

2. The climax.

3. The conclusion.

To access the teaching sessions,
use the instructions in the back
of your Bible study book.

DISCUSS

Use these questions and prompts to discuss the video teaching.

At the end of the teaching video, Ray noted, "We rarely apologize for anything." What do you think about that? Why do you think we tend to struggle with honesty about our mess-ups?

Why is it important that we are honest with God and each other about our mess-ups? What is dangerous about the concealment of sin in relationship with God? In our relationships with other people?

The realness and honesty so openly expressed in the Psalms sometimes shocks us. That might be because we struggle to honestly express our reality to God and other people. But that doesn't let us off the hook. The Psalms are in God's Word to help us move toward deep and honest openness. Psalm 51 is a great example, and Ray offered three insights to help us get the most out of it.

1. The backstory.

Skim through David's backstory in 2 Samuel 11–12. Do these details make it hard for you to understand why God would say that David was "a man after my heart, who will do all my will" (Acts 13:22)? Why?

Now read Psalm 51:1-15. Is it still hard for you to understand why God would make such a statement about David? Why not?

In what ways can all of us relate to David's backstory? In what ways does God want us to relate to David's heart in Psalm 51?

2. The climax.

Read Psalm 51:16-17. Based on David's declaration here, how should we define real repentance before God?

- ☐ remorse
- ☐ good behavior
- ☐ the sacrifice of desires
- ☐ a posture of humility and brokenness
- ☐ an apology

Read Isaiah 57:15. How do we develop a contrite and lowly spirit before God in response to our sin?

How would you counsel someone who wants to know how to go down low in the place of brokenness before God?

3. The conclusion.

Read Psalm 51:18-19. If we understand the phrase "build up the walls" as the morale, cohesion, and unity of the people of God, what responsibility do we each have to our churches when we sin?

Ray asked, "What if true repentance goes viral among us in our generation?" How could that start among us? What challenges would we need to overcome? What benefits would we experience?

What remaining questions or comments do you have about this session's teaching video? What was challenging, convicting, encouraging, or timely for your current circumstances?

CLOSE IN PRAYER

Prayer Requests

PSALM 51

OUTLINE FOR PSALM 51
Introductory petition (1-2)
Lament (3-6)
Major petition (7-12)
Vow of acknowledgment (13-17)
Prayer for the people of God (18-19)

David had sinned. He took another man's wife, got her pregnant, arranged her husband's death, and then for about a year acted like nothing was wrong. Now David was coming back to God with a broken heart. Biblical repentance is not just turning from sin; it is turning back to God, because He is gracious to sinners. In Psalm 51, that's where we find David. He was like the prodigal son (Luke 15:11-32), finally stumbling home to his father, honestly admitting everything.

Read Psalm 51. Why is this psalm personally applicable to every person, not just those who commit sins you consider especially horrible?

Why is confession of sins a necessary part of real faith in Jesus?

The gospel doesn't remove the need for repentance from sins, but provides for that need in Jesus. You can confess your sins, because Jesus died for your sins. However, if you see yourself as above repentance, you know nothing of the gospel (1 John 3:6), and your "Christianity" is your own self-invented religious flattery. The true gospel does not create superior people; the gospel creates people who trust Jesus enough to face themselves honestly and own up.

Read Matthew 11:28. What are some reasons we sometimes lug around a sin God invites us to lay down before Him in confession?

PERSONAL HONESTY

Reread Psalm 51:1-2 and consider what David's words teach you about God and yourself. Record those truths in the columns provided.

Truths About God	Truths About Me

No sinner has ever come to God in confession of sin, recognizing Jesus's mercy, love, and grace on the cross, and been refused—and no one ever will. What we see of ourselves here is transgressions, iniquity, and sin. But God is famous for grace, love, and mercy. *He* is why we can repent. The very sin we'd rather ignore, God wants to blot out. What are you waiting for?

Have you ever struggled with confessing sin and asking forgiveness from those you have wronged, or from God Himself? What underlying wrong beliefs cause that to happen?

Sin must always be seen from God's perspective. He is the one who determines what is and is not sin. Forgiveness is needed to absolve our guilt and restore the broken relationship between us and God. The Bible assures us God is willing to forgive us and to cleanse us from every sin (1 John 1:9), but sometimes we avoid asking God's forgiveness because of our pride. Each one of us has sinned and fallen short of God's design for us (Romans 3:23). When we acknowledge that and honestly confess those sins, we'll always find Him ready to forgive us.

Reread Psalm 51:3-6. What words did David use to describe his sin?

Why are David's blunt words important?

Have you ever thought of your own sin as "evil" and used that word to describe something you've done? Why or why not?

Evil is a humiliating word. When we sin, we would rather say "I messed up" or "I had a bad day." But if God is gracious, loving, and merciful, we can stop lying to ourselves with soft words. True confession and repentance trusts God enough to use blunt words. Recognizing sin as God sees it is the only way to get free.

Reread verses 7-12. What does David ask in each verse?

v. 7

v. 8

v. 9

v. 10

v. 11

v. 12

David isn't afraid he might lose his salvation; he is afraid he might lose his anointing—the blessing of God that accompanied being king. God has put His blessing on His church, and He can take it away—not because He is arbitrary, but because He is principled. God cannot bless hidden, unconfessed, protected sin. And after all, no sin is hidden from God. So let's stay low before the Lord. Let's stay gentle with one another. Let's not insist on winning, but let's always be willing to lose, and the Lord's felt presence will gladly rest upon us.

What is our role in renewal and restoration? What is God's role?

The joy of fellowship with God is one of God's greatest gifts. Loss of that fellowship is the greatest tragedy. For David, God's salvation meant deliverance and freedom from the inner consequences of sin. Sin had bound and burdened him, taking away his energy and hope. When God restored the joy of His salvation, it meant that He had set David free from the burden and guilt of his sin. David could *live* again!

Reread Psalm 51:13-17.

What promises does David make to God in these verses?

Are these same promises part of every person's path of repentance? Why?

What kinds of sacrifices does the Lord desire? How does this help us think more clearly about what repentance is?

What would these sacrifices look like in your life?

David isn't trivializing the sacrifices at the tabernacle. They were acted out predictions of the cross! But he is saying that he could go through all the right motions with a wrong heart. Two things are beautiful to God: the finished work of Christ on the cross, and the broken spirit and contrite heart that embraces the cross. When Jesus forgives us by His blood, we do not high-five Him! Humbled by what we cost Him there, we decide to live fully for Him.

PUBLIC HONESTY

Reread Psalm 51:18-19.

Why are these verses here? Because David was a leader. His personal sins damaged the public cause of the gospel in his generation. "Zion" is the city of God, the socially visible community where Christ lives in the world today. We call it the Christian church. And when David prayed, "Build up the walls of Jerusalem," he meant, "Rebuild the damaged walls"—though not literal walls. He was concerned for people, because his bad example had harmed and damaged the whole cause of Christ.

Why is public repentance needed in the church today?

The need for public repentance is not only for leaders. Every one of us matters. When we personally and publicly confess and repent of our sins, we make the real Jesus non-ignorable. And that is how the walls are repaired.

How does Psalm 51 free you to be honest with God and with yourself?

PSALM 51

REAL HONESTY

Use the spaces below to journal a prayer or response to each prompt.

AUTHENTICITY. Without honesty of confession and repentance before God and others, our lives are marked by hypocrisy—both personally and publicly. But with honesty of confession and repentance before God and others, our lives become recognizable displays of the gospel message. Where do you need greater authenticity before God? Before others?

COMMUNITY. It's not only up to church leaders. Every member of Christ's church is a public figure, standing together side by side in sacred covenant before the Lord for His glory. You aren't hidden. Your voice for Christ rings out loudly. Are you merely present in the community of God's people, or do you actively participate in shared repentance?

TESTIMONY. The "walls" of Christ's church have certainly been damaged—both personally and publicly. But God uses the testimony of our honest confession and repentance to rebuild. You have a story to tell, and that story is meant to help others find hope in the power of the risen Christ.

REVIVAL. We cannot expect revival without first entering into a spirit of honest confession and repentance. And you have a role in that. The advance of the global church will be strengthened through *your* spirit of faith and repentance—by His grace, for His glory.

PSALM 73

OUTLINE OF PSALM 73

The problem: "I was envious of the arrogant" (1-3)

They have it so good (4-12)

Poor me! (13-15)

"Then I discerned . . ." (16-17)

Stupid me! (18-22)

I have it *so* good (23-26)

The privilege: "It is good to be near God" (27-28)

The man who wrote Psalm 73 had wandered from God—not at the level of behavior, but down in his heart. And he was honest about it. His name was Asaph, and he had questions that caused him to nearly lose his faith.

What questions about God, yourself, and the world have you wrestled with at some point in your life?

☐ Why does God let bad things happen to good people?

☐ Why does God allow evil people to succeed?

☐ If God really loves me, then why do I feel so empty?

☐ If the gospel really works, then why do I want to live for myself like everyone else?

☐ Other: _____

Have those questions impacted your faith? How so?

If you've wrestled with those questions or others like them, you're not alone. That's why Psalm 73 is in the Bible. Asaph saw bad people succeeding and good people failing, and it drove him away from God. But God held onto Asaph and helped him, had mercy on him, and changed him. Asaph stumbled his way into richer enjoyment of God than he even knew existed. Psalm 73 is God's breakthrough point for every one of us who is secretly disappointed with God and skeptical that sadness will ever change.

A FAMILIAR PROBLEM

Read Psalm 73:1-12. What was Asaph's problem (vv. 1-3)?

Asaph knew there were faithful people who were experiencing God and enjoying His goodness (v. 1), but he was not one of them (v. 2). He wasn't denying their experience was real, but he didn't feel a connection to that kind of life. Instead, he was drawn to people living God-neglecting lives and wanted to join them (v. 3).

Verses 4-12 describe arrogant and sinful people. Who do you look at with this kind of envy?

Essentially, Asaph concluded, "They have it so good" (v. 12). And we all understand that thought, don't we? The well-off of this world can afford to erect barriers between themselves and the troubles of average folks. If their retirement funds drop 40 percent, they still have tons of money. And what we see in these verses and in our experience is that they got there by *breaking* the rules. In this world, greed and arrogance *succeed*. That's just the way it is. This world does everything wrong, on purpose, and it seems to work.

Read Psalm 73:13-15. How did Asaph view his walk with the Lord? Can you relate?

Asaph felt that he had given up so much for God, and the sacrifice wasn't worth it. But he couldn't *admit* he was thinking this way. He knew his doubts would only upset other people's faith. So he suffered alone. He kept smiling and going to church. But he wouldn't talk about it. That's how he felt. But God had not forsaken him. God met him in a profound way.

Read Psalm 73:16-20. What helped Asaph adjust his perspective? What was he able to discern?

THE CLARITY OF SHOCK

Finally, there came a day when Asaph saw something new. He thought he had looked at the facts, but he hadn't looked at all the facts. He thought he had seen too much of reality, but he hadn't seen enough of reality. Finally, he saw hell: "Then I discerned their end" (v. 17).

What do the following verses teach you about the reality of a life lived apart from God?

Matthew 10:28

Matthew 25:41-46

2 Thessalonians 1:9

Revelation 20:15

Why does God's good news include such honesty about the stark reality of sinful disobedience?

Self-pity distorts reality. We talk ourselves into grievance. If all you can see is this present world, you *will* become bitter. But who envies the elegant rich as they board the luxury liner *Titanic*? In verses 1-15, the psalmist looked at this world; then something changed and he saw the world with shock. Envy had warped his perception. He had been deceived by appearances, but then he started breaking through to reality. Asaph started changing, and so can we. Godly shock gave Asaph *clarity*.

What are you able to see better when you are looking first at God?

Read Psalm 73:21-26. What was Asaph's honest assessment of himself?

What was his newfound honest assessment of God?

Asaph's problem was his own "brutish" heart toward God (v. 22). God gave Asaph three seconds of insight into hell, which is better than three years of classes in seminary. He woke up. He went into repentance. Asaph finally got it. He saw his life in a new, truthful way—with a sense of wonder and privilege before God.

With His strength in our weakness, God continually guides us. What is your role in that process?

What truths about God in these verses stand out to you most personally in your current circumstance? Why?

Even when we are stubborn, God is still holding onto us. Our crises do not overthrow His mercies. His strong commitment to us is more lasting than our flimsy commitment to Him. He has determined to draw us away from envy of this world into desire for Himself, and He will not be denied.

Read Psalm 73:27-28.

What good purpose does God intend in your life when you experience evil and suffering in this world?

Contrast verses 15 and 28. What was Asaph ready to talk about? Why?

Why should a fresh encounter with God always result in public testimony?

This man was a silent doubter; now he was a vocal worshiper. God wants you to make the same transition today. Here's the key—Jesus died to give you *God* forever.

What do the following verses teach you about God's purposes in your questions?

1 Peter 3:18

Psalm 16:11

Philippians 3:8

When God wins our hearts this way, the disciplines of holiness no longer feel like deprivation; they become a feast of enjoying God.

PSALM 73
REAL HONESTY

Use the spaces below to journal a prayer or response to each prompt.

FREEDOM. Asaph was honest. He told God and us about his real struggles. When that kind of honesty spreads out into a church, the help that everyone feels goes up exponentially. What questions or hang-ups do you need to confess to God and His people in honesty so that you might receive His rest?

PRACTICALITY. Asaph was practical. He was not interested in the finer points of Bible interpretation. He wanted God to be real to him. Do you? If you desire God, you're feeling the most profound desire of all.

RELIEF. Maybe the most important word in all the psalm is the word "until" in verse 17. Asaph was in secret anguish—*until* God met him. If you are frustrated with God, don't give up. Cry out to Him, and He will schedule into your life an "until," when He meets you in a new way.

CHANGE. Asaph went from envy of the arrogant (v. 3) to desire for God (v. 25). What changed was his emotions. Do you believe in God, but lack desire for God? Are you are envious of this world, secretly angry that God isn't giving you the designer life you had in mind? Be honest about that, and invite God to melt your hardened heart. He will.

PSALMS OF PERSONAL LAMENT

As Ray explained in Going Deeper, the gospel doesn't deny or suppress our sadness; rather, it invites us to bring our most keenly felt sadness to Christ. The psalms of lament help us *see* our real needs and *bring* them to our real Savior with honesty, transparency, and vulnerability.

As a way of engaging with God in that way, consider another psalm of lament,
Psalm 13, in light of the three questions given in the Going Deeper video teaching.

How long, O LORD? Will you forget me forever?

How long will you hide your face from me?

How long must I take counsel in my soul

and have sorrow in my heart all the day?

How long shall my enemy be exalted over me?

Consider and answer me, O LORD my God;

light up my eyes, lest I sleep the sleep of death,

lest my enemy say, "I have prevailed over him,"

lest my foes rejoice because I am shaken.

But I have trusted in your steadfast love;

my heart shall rejoice in your salvation.

I will sing to the LORD,

because he has dealt bountifully with me.

What is my crisis?

What crisis was the psalmist facing?

What similar crisis have I faced or am I facing now?

Who is my Savior above my crisis?

Who did the psalmist understand God to be in this crisis, even though he didn't yet feel or experience God in that way?

Who do you know God to be in your crisis, even if you don't yet feel or experience Him as such?

How do the Psalms connect my crisis with my Savior?

Personalizing Psalm 13, how should you connect with Jesus in this crisis?

To access the teaching sessions, use the instructions in the back of your Bible study book.

REAL HOPE

GROUP STUDY

START

*Welcome the group to session 4, "Real Hope." Before introducing
session 4, take a few minutes to review session 3.*

Before we dig into this week's study on the real hope we find in the Psalms, let's discuss what we learned last week. In our personal study, we discovered how the Psalms help us lean into real honesty with God and each other.

What real-life issues did your study of Psalms 51 and 73 address for you?

What help in those real-life issues did Psalms 51 and 73 offer you?

How did the questions in Going Deeper help you better understand how the psalms of lament benefit you? How might considering those questions as you read the Psalms help you see your needs and bring them to Jesus with honesty, transparency, and vulnerability?

In sin and hardship, honesty before the Lord and other believers can feel daunting. But, as we'll discover this week, God's Word doesn't invite that kind of vulnerability without also providing us the hope we need.

In what current situation do you need God's help of real hope?

*To prepare for video session 4, pray that God will help
each person understand and apply this truth:*

God loves to give His best to sinners
who deserve the worst.

WATCH

Use these statements to follow along as you watch video session 4.

To get the most out of Psalm 85, consider these three insights:

1. The structure.

2. Words of wrath.

3. Key words.

To access the teaching sessions,
use the instructions in the back
of your Bible study book.

DISCUSS

Use these questions and prompts to discuss the video teaching.

Ray began and ended the teaching video by telling us that God loves to give His best to people who deserve His worst. The tension in that is that most people don't view themselves as deserving God's worst. In fact, when we heard that God loves to give His best to people who deserve His worst, our thoughts might have automatically turned outward to people who do especially horrible things. That's because we tend to think we have the capacity to deserve God's goodness, and then work to achieve it.

Why is there no hope in our good works?

Why is the starting point of real hope found in the place of realization that we don't deserve God's best, we deserve God's worst?

Psalm 85 doesn't minimize or ignore our sin or our need. Rather, it is honest about the great chasm between who God is and who we are. In doing so, it helps us find the real hope God offers. Let's discuss the three insights Ray pointed out to help us get the most out of Psalm 85.

1. The structure.

What grace has God given us all in the past (vv. 1-3)?

What need do we all have in the present (vv. 4-7)?

What clarity and resolve can we all have in the present (vv. 8-9)?

What future grace does God promise all who trust in Jesus (vv. 10-13)?

2. Words of wrath.

Is it hard for you to read about God's wrath (v. 3), hot anger (v. 3), and indignation (v. 4) in the Psalms? Has that kind of terminology ever made you fear or doubt the hope you have in Christ Jesus? Explain.

Read Hebrews 12:7-11. What hope is there for believers in the wrath, or discipline, of God?

Reread Psalm 85:6. What connection is there between discipline and revival? How have you experienced this in your own life?

3. Key words.

Ray pointed out key words that appear throughout Psalm 85 like *revive* (v. 6), *again* (vv. 4,6), *steadfast love and faithfulness* (v. 10), *folly* (v. 8), and *fear* (v. 9). Which of these words, or what other word in Psalm 85, opens up the whole psalm for you most personally? In what way?

What remaining questions or comments do you have about this session's teaching video? What was challenging, convicting, encouraging, or timely for your current circumstances?

CLOSE IN PRAYER

Prayer Requests

PSALM 85

OUTLINE FOR PSALM 85
Grace in the past: gratitude (1-3)
Need in the present: urgency (4-7)
Resolve in the present: clarity (8-9)
Grace in the future: expectancy (10-13)

Whatever came to mind when you first read this study title, *Real Help for Real Life*, maybe what you are finding is this: what matters for you isn't a long list, and it isn't complicated. It's a spirit of discovery (Psalms 1 and 2)—you can know God, not hypothetically or only as doctrine, but as personal and present, moment by moment. It is a spirit of rest (Psalms 23 and 130)—relating to God as real in a world impressed with itself. It is a spirit of repentance (Psalms 51 and 73)—staying honest and low before Him about our sins and betrayals. And, this week, we'll see that it is also a spirit of hope.

THE NEED FOR HOPE

Why does hope seems elusive to many people in the world today?

What are some ways people try to combat feelings of mental or emotional exhaustion and attempt to grab onto hope?

None of us enjoys being dead and bored and hardened. Going back to Jesus for newness of life and hope in a world of exhaustion is a sacred reality that is universal, powerful, and life-giving. This is why the risen Jesus's bold claim in Revelation 1:18 resonates in our hearts today: "I am *the living one*." In other words, "Y'all are half dead. But I am the living one, from whom all life flows. Let me love you back to life—over and over again!" And that is the whole point of Psalm 85—*life*!

THE REALITY OF HOPE

LORD, you were favorable to your land;
>   you restored the fortunes of Jacob.
You forgave the iniquity of your people;
>   you covered all their sin.
You withdrew all your wrath;
>   you turned from your hot anger.

PSALM 85:1-3

What do these verses teach you about God?

Many of us can look back on a moment when we were fed up with ourselves, but God forgave us, He got us back on track, and life began working again. But after a while, temptation was strong, we were weak, and we messed up our lives *again*. That's why Psalm 85 is in the Bible. We have all proven how we can be reckless all over again—even after God has been good to us. *What hope do we have then?*

What hope do these verses offer, even when you have carelessly abused God's grace?

Psalm 85 is for people like us who are out of excuses, scared that our chance at life might be over, with no one to blame but ourselves, heartsick over the mess we've made, but looking back up to God again. Psalm 85 is in the Bible for that moment—when we need life and hope and a future only God can give and sustain. Psalm 85 is saying, that's revival, and God loves to give it.

What is the relationship between gratitude for God's past grace and hope for the future?

HEAR WHAT THE LORD WILL SPEAK

Restore us again, O God of our salvation,
    and put away your indignation toward us!
Will you be angry with us forever?
    Will you prolong your anger to all generations?
Will you not revive us again,
    that your people may rejoice in you?
Show us your steadfast love, O LORD,
    and grant us your salvation.

PSALM 85:4-7

What present need did the psalmist express to God?

Do you sense that your situation is really this urgent? Should you? Explain.

What is the danger in not recognizing that our sin poses an urgent need?

In verses 4-9, we do serious business with God. We ask Him for the impossible, because He's good at it. We ask Him for a miracle, because He loves hopeless cases. We ask Him to give us our lives back, and He gives us far better.

> Let me hear what God the LORD will speak,
>> for he will speak peace to his people, to his saints;
>> but let them not turn back to folly.
> Surely his salvation is near to those who fear him,
>> that glory may dwell in our land.

PSALM 85:8-9

For what reason does God always provide in our hopelessness?

Have you ever struggled to have clarity about the hope God provides? Why does that happen to us?

We think we have X number of chances with God. And when we've clipped all our coupons, it's over. But that whole way of thinking is wrong. It's not about us being good enough to keep God cooperative. That is not how God thinks. It's about us hearing from God. He announces our hope. The gospel tells us that Jesus bled and died on the cross for all our inexcusable betrayals, and His death really and fully paid for it all. So we *can* run back to God every time we sin, knowing His arms are open. What matters to Him is not what we deserve but that Jesus died for us, the undeserving.

What is your role in receiving a spirit of hope? How can you stay open to the promise of hope?

HOPE IN GRACE

Steadfast love and faithfulness meet;
    righteousness and peace kiss each other.
Faithfulness springs up from the ground,
    and righteousness looks down from the sky.
Yes, the LORD will give what is good,
    and our land will yield its increase.
Righteousness will go before him
    and make his footsteps a way.

PSALM 85:10-13

What imagery stands out to you in these verses?

What is your understanding of its meaning?

The picture here is one of new and miraculous harmony, fullness, freshness, and abundant grace, with nothing stopping God or even slowing him down. *That's* your future in Christ. He doesn't just patch you up a little here and there. He gives you a whole new reality. You get your *life* back, far better than before.

The risen Christ knows how to give sinners a future that leaves us thinking, "Look what *God* has done!" It takes poetry, like these beautiful verses, to describe what only God can do, and what God does for damaged people—both because they have sinned and because they have been sinned against. God lifts us up into the overflowing glory of the risen Jesus, who is moving through the world today with healing and life and joy. He alone gives us a spirit of soaring hope.

PSALM 85
REAL HOPE

Use the spaces below to journal a prayer or response to each prompt.

RENEWAL. Verse 6 asks, "Will you not revive us again?" We run down and wear out. We can't live today on what God gave yesterday. Our needs are endless, but so is His newness. What matters most is not us, but Him. Jesus did not come to make death more palatable; He came to give life more abundant (John 10:10). Will you let Him breathe new life into you, that you may rejoice in Him?

SECOND CHANCES. Another key word in verse 6 is "again." That doesn't mean the renewal they received before wasn't real. It means they squandered it. We've all done it—again and again. That's why we need Him to revive us *again*. For every "again" of our sin, there is an even greater "again" of His grace. Never lose hope! Keep coming back to Jesus, however many times you stray. His arms are open to you now.

EXPECTATION. The word *folly* in verse 8 means a lack of openness, not a lack of intelligence. It's a complacency born from indifference. It can start excusing anything, because eagerness has died. The resolve to keep paying attention, though, is clear: "Let me hear!" You can pay attention, or not pay attention—run to Jesus, or dawdle along the way. That choice is the key to your future. True expectation is about being fully open to receive His glory in the gospel sung, the gospel prayed, the gospel preached, the gospel shared, and the gospel sent out.

PSALM 42/43

OUTLINE FOR PSALM 42/43

Dry (42:1-5)

Drowning (42:6-11)

Distressed (43:1-5)

For reasons we don't know, this one psalm was divided into two as it was copied through the centuries. But what we need is the message of the whole psalm. Psalm 42/43 is a believing, tenacious, honest, hopeful lament.

> **Do the words "hopeful" and "lament" seem complementary or conflicting to you? Why?**

REACHING FOR JOY

Read Psalm 42/43.

Christian believers understand sorrow. They always have. The apostle Peter described normal Christian experience in these two modes—being grieved by various trials, and rejoicing with joy inexpressible (1 Peter 1:6,8). The psalmist here was sinking down into grief but fighting back with hope-filled faith.

> **Currently, what resonates with you most as you read this psalm: grief, hope, or a mix of the two? Why?**

Psalm 42/43 teaches us how to keep reaching for joy. The poet was both overwhelmingly distressed and ruggedly hopeful. He moves back and forth from one to the other, because real-life Christianity is not a simplistic success story. It's a battle, with defeats and victories along the way, but with the power of God preserving us in the fight.

> **Reread Psalm 42:1-5. Has there ever been a time in your life when you felt like you were in a spiritual drought? What did you do to find remedy?**

The deer understands thirst. He feels it in every cell of his body. And the believer understands one need at the center of his or her existence: the living God. If we have counselors, doctors, and sympathetic friends, good. But only God satisfies our deepest longings—and not just God, but the nearness of God (v. 2). Do not accept any other assessment of your need. You, yes you, might need some vacation. You might need to thin out your overcommitted schedule. But you could do all that and you'd still be this deer dying of thirst, because you were made for *God*.

> **Verse 3 gives some insight as to why we often struggle to trust God as the only answer to the dryness we feel in our souls. What is it?**

> **What do you look to and trust instead?**

> **From verses 4-5, what did the psalmist do to fight back?**

The psalmist didn't listen to himself; he spoke to himself. He didn't trust himself; he defied himself. He didn't accept his thoughts; he announced the gospel to his thoughts, and not the gospel in generalities but the gospel applied personally to him: "Hope in God; for I shall again praise him, my salvation and my God." *He preached hope to himself.* And every one of us is called to be this kind of preacher.

HOPE IN GOD

Read the following verses and jot down what promises God has lovingly given you to hang onto when everything else gives way and lets you down:

1 Peter 5:7

John 16:33

Hebrews 13:5

Genesis 15:1

Matthew 11:28

> Hope in God; for I shall again praise him.
> **PSALM 42:5**

Knowing the promises of God, *what* was the psalmist longing for? What did he set his heart on?

The refreshment he longed for was not strolling along some Caribbean beach or a weekend to binge-watch his favorite series; he wanted to get back into public worship. It is not only a great privilege to have a church to come to every Lord's Day, it is a God-appointed refreshing. This remedy is so simple, we might overlook it. But God doesn't. Jesus said, "Where two or three are gathered in my name, there am I among them" (Matthew 18:20).

Reread Psalm 42:6-11. In verse 5 the psalmist challenged his downcast soul. What happens next in verse 6? What does this tell you about the nature of grief?

The psalmist wasn't only feeling dry—now we see he was also drowning. But what did he recognize about God in his drowning?

We can see God even in the waves of discouragement that threaten to overwhelm us. They are "your waterfalls, your breakers, your waves." God hates the isolation we suffer, the taunting unbelief and the overflowing sadness, but He is also involved in it. Dig deeply enough, and we eventually find God's love at work.

A SONG IN THE SORROW

By day the LORD commands his steadfast love,
and at night his song is with me,
a prayer to the God of my life.

PSALM 42:8

Verse 8 is the centerpiece of the whole psalm. The heart of the psalm is the heart of our existence—God commanding His steadfast love, bringing a song, a prayer, to make every moment of our lives one more masterstroke on the canvas of His redemptive art.

God commands His steadfast love to bring a song into your heart, even when you feel like you're drowning. What is your role in receiving it?

Why can't other people heal our wounds?

Even as the psalmist lost his footing under those waves and breakers and felt forgotten by God (v. 9), he also knew that God was the rock under his feet. He had been deeply wounded, but he also knew that stab of mockery (v. 10) wasn't telling him the truth. And so he shook himself awake once again in verse 11. He deliberately turned his eyes back to the joy set before him—the public, corporate worship of God.

> **Reread Psalm 43. What truth did the accusations of other people cause the psalmist to question?**

The accusations of others can darken our own thoughts of God. Our brains are remarkably ready to rush to the worst conclusions. But as the psalmist was lost and wandering around in his despair, he taught us how to pray when we find ourselves out there in that state of despair.

> **In your own words, what was the psalmist asking God to do in verse 3?**

He was not angry at God. He knew that God was his exceeding joy. And in praying this way, the psalmist raised a question for us all: Do we *want* to be found? Just that desire, the weakest openness, is enough for God. The psalmist moved all his chips over onto that square. Will you?

> Why are you cast down, O my soul,
>   and why are you in turmoil within me?
> Hope in God; for I shall again praise him,
>   my salvation and my God.
>
> **PSALM 43:5**

PSALM 42/43

REAL HOPE

Use the spaces below to journal a prayer or response to each prompt.

PERSPECTIVE. A darkness came over Jesus that we have never experienced, and He endured it for us. He took on our guilt and misery. He took it all to His cross, where God put it away forever. Will you still suffer? Yes. But if you are in Christ, your sin and your misery do not diminish God's love for you, and they do not define your future, because God's wrath was poured out on that cross in the most godforsaken experience ever. So your own self-punishment cannot atone for you. What breathes life into you is looking to Jesus.

IDENTITY. When you're in despair, God is not in despair over you. He has put His hand on you with a purpose of grace. Your life will be defined not by your turbulent doubts but by God's steadfast love.

SURPRISE. If you aren't delighting in Christ today, that doesn't mean you can't have real hope. It means God is taking you deeper, as you mourn the loss of His felt presence in your heart and seek Him afresh. Bring your sadness to Him. Even if all you have is the tiniest particle of faith, the size of a mustard seed, God will move mountains with it (Matthew 17:20). He'll surprise you. It's His promise. Why not believe it?

PSALMS AS A DAILY RESOURCE

You're more than halfway through this study in the Psalms, and likely gaining new insights every day. That's great! At the same time, we can look forward, too. As we learned in this week's Going Deeper, the valuable benefit you gain from the Psalms does not have to end when you complete the final pages of this book. The Psalms are meant to be a daily resource for the rest of your life.

Based on the three suggestions Ray gave in this week's Going Deeper video, begin making a plan to use the Psalms as a daily resource.

Make a plan and follow the plan.

Create a plan for reading the Psalms each day. (For example, start in Psalm 1 and read one psalm each day for the next six months. Repeat.)

At what point in the day will you read the Psalms? In what specific place will you read the Psalms each day? What distractions will you need to remove to gain clear focus as you read the Psalms each day?

Have a companion.

What commentary will you use to enrich your study of the Psalms?

Who is someone with whom you can discuss what you're learning?

Dare to believe what you're discovering.

What situation are you facing that you need to apply the Psalms to, defying darkness and walking in the light of Christ?

Take some time now to practice using the Psalms as a daily resource. Starting in the chapter that aligns with your newly formed plan, read God's Word in the place you have chosen. Read commentary that gives you insight into that psalm. Acknowledge how you need to apply the psalm in real life, daring to believe what you've discovered. As you walk through that process, record your thoughts, questions, and prayers in the space below.

To access the teaching sessions, use the instructions in the back of your Bible study book.

REAL

COURAGE

GROUP STUDY

START

Welcome the group to session 5, Real Courage.
Before introducing session 5, take a few minutes to review session 4.

In our personal study last week, we discovered how the Psalms help us know and live with real hope. Let's discuss together some of the insights we gained.

What real-life issues did Psalms 85 and 42/43 address for you?

What real help in those real-life issues did Psalms 85 and 42/43 offer you?

What plan did you make to use the Psalms as a daily resource? What commentary will you use to enrich your study of the Psalms? How might using the Psalms as a daily resource help you believe and walk in hope?

Knowing the hope of Christ compels us to walk in that hope. In other words, the hope of the gospel applies itself in real life. This week, we'll take a look at the everyday practicality of a spirit of hope, discovery, rest, and honesty—real courage.

In what current situation do you need to demonstrate real courage?

To prepare for video session 5, pray that God will help
each person understand and apply this truth:

If we have the courage to face Jesus,
we can face everything else.

WATCH

Use these statements to follow along as you watch video session 5.

Three things to notice about Psalm 139:

1. Hatred in verses 21-22—"I hate them with complete hatred."

2. Pivot in verse 18—"I awake, and I am still with you."

3. Courage throughout verses 1-24—"You have searched me and known me. . . . Where shall I flee from your presence? . . . You knitted me together in my mother's womb. . . . Lead me in the way everlasting!"

To access the teaching sessions, use the instructions in the back of your Bible study book.

DISCUSS

Use these questions and prompts to discuss the video teaching.

Read Psalm 139.

This is a familiar and often quoted text. What topics have you previously considered within the context of this psalm?

How do these topics relate to our topic of real courage?

Psalm 139 speaks to important and debated topics in culture today like abortion, gender identity, and the sanctity of life. As such, it is possible that many of us have read Psalm 139 numerous times without realizing that David's context was personal suffering at the hands of evil adversaries. In that suffering, the knowledge of God's gracious involvement and loving purposes gave David *courage*. Psalm 139 is in the Bible to renew our courage, too. So let's talk through the three insights Ray offered, as a way of helping us get the most out of Psalm 139.

1. Hatred in verses 21-22—"I hate them with complete hatred."

   Read Proverbs 6:16-19, Proverbs 8:13, Psalm 11:5, Psalm 26:5, Matthew 5:43-44, Proverbs 10:12, and Romans 12:9. What do these verses teach us about hate? About God? About following Him in a world like this?

   Ray said, "Let's be open to God correcting evil in us, and let's stand against evil wherever else we find it." What struggle is there in either of those two applications of real courage?

2. Pivot in verse 18—"I awake, and I am still with you."

   How do you answer the question, "What can you absolutely count on right now?"

How can God's knowledge of you (1-6), presence with you (7-12), and formation of you (13-18) inspire and support you when your back is against the wall?

When David wrote Psalm 139, his back *was* against the wall. He was suffering. Enemies opposed him. But as he considered who *God* is, he began to see his suffering from a different perspective. His circumstances hadn't changed, and he was still in danger. At the same time, *everything* had changed because he was still in the presence of the Lord. God knew him, God was with him, and God had made him, so David was ready to courageously face any path to which God might lead him. Are we?

3. Courage throughout verses 1-24—"You have searched me and known me. . . . Where shall I flee from your presence? . . . You knitted me together in my mother's womb. . . . Lead me in the way everlasting!"

Reread Psalm 139:23-24. Respond to the following statement Ray made: "If we have the courage to face the Lord Jesus, we can face everything else."

What would it look like for us to live courageously in Christ this week?

What remaining questions or comments do you have about this session's teaching video? What was challenging, convicting, encouraging, or timely for your current circumstances?

CLOSE IN PRAYER

Prayer Requests

PSALM 139

OUTLINE FOR PSALM 139

Lord, you know me (1-6)

Lord, you are with me (7-12)

Lord, you made me (13-18a)

[pivot from meditation to alertness: 18b]

Lord, I'm for you! (19-24)

C. S. Lewis said, "Courage is not simply *one* of the virtues but the form of every virtue at the testing point."[1] In other words, courage is the real-world *application* of discovery, rest, honesty, hope, and every other help God's Spirit pours into our lives. For example, the spirit of discovery in Psalm 1 and 2 is courage trusting the living God and conquering King. The spirit of rest in Psalm 23 and 130 is courage treating Jesus as real in trouble. The spirit of repentance in Psalm 51 and 73 is courage owning up to our sins. The spirit of hope in Psalm 85 and 42/43 is courage praying for a better future. In this week's study, we see, at a practical level, the key to it all.

> **What is a promise of God that you struggle to personally apply? What fear do you think causes that struggle in you?**

In today's psalm, we see a scared believer going to God and hanging on. And that scared believer ends up receiving from God the clarity and the decisiveness for his next step.

Courage is a major theme in the Bible. How could it be otherwise? This world, where we're trying to follow Jesus, is no friend to Jesus. We need courage every day, and Psalm 139 offers us a strong place to stand.

1. C. S. Lewis, *The Screwtape Letters* (San Francisco: Harper Collins, 2001), 161.

Read Psalm 139:1-6. Some think it is a fearful thing to be searched and known by God. What about you? How do you feel knowing that God completely knows your activity, thoughts, path, words, and intentions?

COURAGE FROM AWARENESS

In Psalm 139, David wasn't sitting around a campfire making s'mores and having the time of his life. He was in trouble. Everything was on the line, and his life was hanging by a thread. Bad guys were after him. David drew the ire of Saul and others because he stood for Christ among powerful people who stood against Christ. He desperately needed courage.

Where did David find that courage? He reconnected with what he could count on. He might have actually been sitting around a campfire at night far out in the desert. But if so, we should picture him deep in thought. As he sat there, David allowed himself to savor the unseen realities of God's involvement with him.

In His complete intimate knowledge of the good, the bad, and everything in between, how did God respond to David (v. 5)?

Why is God's complete knowledge of everything about you "wonderful"?

How can God's knowledge of you give you courage?

Read Psalm 139:7-16. What else did David ponder about God's nature?

For what reasons would the God of the universe choose to be intimately involved in the details of your life?

God is more than simply *aware* of every detail of our lives—He is involved. He is not looking down at us from His throne in heaven and shaking His head or throwing His hands up in disgust, wondering how we could possibly have gotten ourselves into to such a sad state. No, He is ever present with us. God did not knit us together in the womb and then, at birth, set us off to figure it out on our own. As dependent as we are on Him for the creation of life, we are equally dependent on Him to sustain that life. And He does! He loves us, and He is intimately involved with us, even in the most desperate moments of our lives.

What promise is there for you in verses 11-12?

Reread Psalm 139:17-24.

How did David describe His need for God in verses 17-18?

One hang-up many people have with reading the Bible is that God seems impossible for them to grasp. They reason, "Why even try?" David expressed a different message here. What is that message?

COURAGE FROM DEPENDENCE

David completed his meditations in the first part of verse 18—"If I would count them [God's loving thoughts and purposes], they are more than the sand." Instead of feeling precarious, David now felt emboldened, because he knew he was loved and cared for by no one less than almighty God.

What is the connection between the study of Scripture and courage?

From verses 19-24, what courage did David find in meditating on God's character?

Why do we struggle to take a stand against sin? Why must we take a stand against sin?

David was not repulsed for personal or selfish reasons. These verses in Psalm 139 weren't simply David having a bad day. No, he was courageously calling down the righteous judgment of God on powerful men who were rising up against God's ways for their oppressive advantage.

COURAGE FROM CONFESSION

In your own words, what did David ask of God in verses 23-24?

David knew the evil he saw "out there" was also lurking "in here." So he bared his soul before God: "They're wrong. I can see that. But how am *I* wrong? I can't see that. So, Lord, correct me too!" And isn't David's *humility* the reason he rejects evil, including his own?

> **Courage isn't often thought to be joined with humility. Why is humility a necessity for the kind of real courage we find in the Psalms and throughout God's Word?**

> **What do the following verses teach you about what it means to apply a spirit of courage in daily life?**

> > 1 Corinthians 10:13

> > James 4:7

> > 1 John 1:8-10

> > 1 John 3:6-10

> **Why does facing Jesus with your sins give you the courage you need to face everything else?**

PSALM 139
REAL COURAGE

Use the spaces below to journal a prayer or response to each prompt.

PROVISION. You don't have to muster up the courage you need on your own. Everything you need to follow Jesus comes to you freely from Jesus. Turn to Him. Ask Him to search you and know your heart and lead you in the everlasting way. He will do it, and as He does, He will fill you with His courage.

VICTORY. As you follow Jesus, sometimes you might go through living hell. But as you finally emerge from horrible suffering, you find yourself believing in His love for you *more* than you did before you entered into the suffering. You don't merely survive; you are *more* than a conqueror, through Jesus's love (Romans 8:37).

HAPPINESS. In this world you'll get bruised and bloodied and beaten up—and happier. That's because Jesus loves you onto the hard path of following Him, all along the path one step at a time, and keeps loving you all the way into the future. The further you go into His love, care, and provision for you, the more you love Him, and the more true happiness you discover.

PSALM 27

OUTLINE FOR PSALM 27

Confidence in God's faithfulness (1–3)

Request for God's protection (4–6)

Request for God's presence (7–12)

Courage from God's faithfulness (13–14)

We're being reminded in our study of the Psalms that what we believe about God is the most important thing about us. Think about it. David didn't face lions and giants with courage because he was just a really macho guy. He didn't find courage when powerful people were hunting him down to kill him because he was just optimistic by nature. No, David found courage because he believed that God knows everything and was always with him, working all things together according to His purpose. David acted courageously because he had decided in his heart to join God in that purpose. David was a man after God's heart (Acts 13:22).

Would you describe yourself as a person after God's own heart? Why or why not?

What are some practical steps you can take toward a deep and genuine relationship with Christ?

Read Psalm 27. As you consider your own need for courage, record any phrase or statement from the psalm that stands out to you about that.

From verses 1-3, what reasons did David have for confidence and courage?

COURAGE FROM PAST FAITHFULNESS

To begin Psalm 27, David shared an incredible testimony of God's faithfulness. He didn't use hyperbole for the sake of emphasis—several translations set verse 2 in the past tense. God had actually saved him from an army of evil men who were moving toward him like wild animals ready to devour his seemingly lifeless body. There was no way out, except for the grace of God, and David knew it. There were times in the past when the Lord alone had protected David's life.

Name some ways God has shown His faithfulness to you in the past.

How might remembering God's past faithfulness give us courage to face our present fears?

After remembering who God is (v. 1) and what He had done (v. 2), David looked to the uncertain future with confidence (v. 3). Even in the worst-case scenario—even if an army rose up against him and circled around him—David wouldn't be afraid. He would know in his heart that God was for him and completely able to save him.

It's easy to think about everything that goes wrong in life and focus on that. We're not usually focused on the past; we're focused on whatever present uncertainty and future fear stands before us. Though it might be harder to focus our thoughts on the many ways God has protected us and provided for us in the past, that practice is courage-giving. Specifically acknowledging God's faithfulness in the past allowed David to face the future with courageous faith in God's ability to deliver him from any situation.

COURAGE FOR THE FUTURE

Reread Psalm 27:4-6. What was David's one desire for the future?

Considering his circumstances, what are some other desires he might have asked for instead?

In regard to courage, why does it matter what your primary future desire from the Lord is?

The imagery of the temple and tabernacle are central to David's words, because they represented the presence of God on earth throughout the Old Testament. All David wanted was to be in God's presence because he knew that was the safest place to be. And the same is true for us. In any situation, our primary need is not a change in circumstance or human intervention or better effort or a new self-help strategy. God's presence with us is our greatest defense and sole reason for courage. He hides us from our enemy, shields us from attack, and gives us a solid place to stand.

One thing have I asked of the LORD,
    that will I seek after:
that I may dwell in the house of the LORD
    all the days of my life,
to gaze upon the beauty of the LORD
    and to inquire in his temple.

PSALM 27:4

Read Psalm 27:7-12. David shifted from confidently praising God for his future (v. 6) to again pleading with God to deliver him (vv. 7-9). What does that tell us about finding courage?

David knew the power of salvation belongs to the Lord alone (v. 12). So why did he also ask God to teach him how to live and lead him on a level path (v. 11)?

How might knowing how God wants you to live give you courage?

David's troubles hadn't ended—there was surely more to come. He knew his enemies would return and, when they did, he wasn't going to be any more capable to escape their terror. Even his closest relationships failed him (v. 10). His strength and courage were wholly dependent on God, and always would be.

Faith is not merely a decision that we make one time in life. Courage is not something we need only once in awhile. Courageous faith is something we must receive daily. God wants us to actively trust Him every day to provide for us, deliver us from temptation, and grow in our affection for Him. As we continually turn to Him, He shows us that His perfect and unconditional love will never disappoint us.

What changes might take place in your life this week if you were to fully and truly believe that God will never let you down?

How has God comforted you when others let you down?

I believe that I shall look upon the
goodness of the LORD
   in the land of the living!
Wait for the LORD;
   be strong, and let your heart take courage;
   wait for the LORD!

PSALM 27:13-14

How should the hope of eternity impact your life today?

David's situation was a mess, but he didn't use that mess to deny God's goodness in his life—in fact, it was quite the opposite. He clung to the assurance that, despite the sorrow of this world, he would stand in the fullness of God's goodness in the future. Because of this firm belief, David would wait, be strong, and take courage. Why not you too?

Psalm 27 ends by making the same point with which we began—what you believe about God is the most important thing about you. If you don't have a right view of the life to come, then the circumstances of this life will cause you to flounder in despair. Only when you take refuge in Jesus will you know eternal safety. The hope of eternal security—the fact that you will one day finally look Jesus in the face—reorients the way you approach each day this side of heaven. What you believe about God's goodness in the life to come empowers you with the courage to trust Him in the here and now.

In what situation do you need to wait for the Lord, be strong, and let your heart take courage? How does Psalm 27 encourage you in that?

PSALM 27

REAL COURAGE

Use the spaces below to journal a prayer or response to each prompt.

LIGHT. This is a dark world. If you focus on that darkness, there is much to fear. But when you turn to the Lord, He lights your way. He is your salvation and the strength you need to face literally anything that comes your way. And when Christ is your light, salvation, and strength, what darkness do you have to fear?

PRESENCE. One day, every person who trusts in Jesus Christ will enjoy the fullness of His presence in heaven. But, for those same people who trust in Christ, eternity has already begun. He hides you in His shelter, lifts you up, and sets your feet on a rock, even now. His presence is why you *can* seek His face!

DIRECTION. In times of trouble, it is good to sit with a trusted friend. But Jesus doesn't only offer you His presence. If you let Him, He will lead your way, and set you on a firm path.

BELIEF. If your circumstances change your belief, then your "belief" is really something lesser. True belief in God reveals itself in waiting for God. What do you *believe* about God? Be strong and take courage, because He never changes.

READING THE PSALMS FOR GOSPEL INSIGHT

The Psalms, as with all of Scripture, tell God's redemption story. And that is the very best real help for real life the Psalms offer us! Each chapter helps us connect the grace of God and the law of God. In doing so, the Psalms point us to Christ.

Consider Psalm 27 in light of the two sets of concentric circles that Ray described in this week's Going Deeper video. Examine the diagram of grace conditioned by law on this page, given as an example.

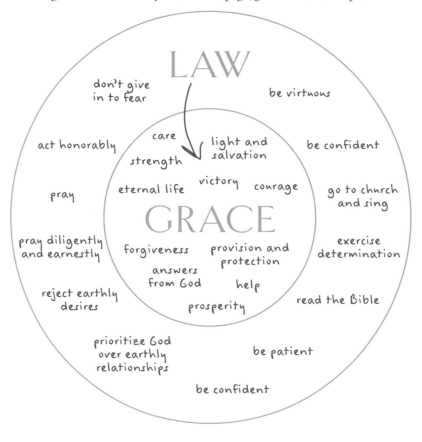

Why is reading Psalm 27 in this way inaccurate?

Next, fill in the circles on page 107 to reflect the law conditioned by grace in Psalm 27.

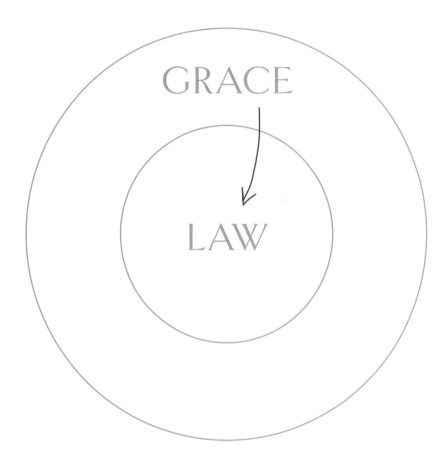

As Ray explained, the New Testament is the best commentary on the Old Testament ever written. We are meant to enter the law of God through the grace of Christ, as the concentric circles on this page show (Galatians 2:19-21).

How does reading Psalm 27 in this way (where the law is conditioned by grace) impact your understanding of Psalm 27?

To access the teaching sessions, use the instructions in the back of your Bible study book.

REAL JOY

GROUP STUDY

START

Welcome the group to session 6, "Real Joy."
Before introducing session 6, take a few minutes to review session 5.

We've made it to the final session of *Psalms: Real Help for Real Life*. This week, we'll complete our study in the most uplifting way—learning what it means to grow in a spirit of real joy! Before we jump in, let's review last week's study on real courage a bit.

What real-life issues did your study of Psalms 139 and 27 address for you?

What help in those issues do Psalms 139 and 27 offer you?

How did the activity using concentric circles in Going Deeper help you better understand how to read the Psalms for gospel insight?

As God speaks to us through the Psalms, He freely and generously develops in us a spirit of discovery, a spirit of rest, a spirit of honesty, a spirit of hope, and a spirit of courage. In this week's study, we'll examine one more real help for real life that flows from all the rest—a spirit of real joy!

In what current situation do you need to grow in the experience and demonstration of real joy?

To prepare for video session 6, pray that God will help each person understand and apply this truth:

A spirit of praise to God is our better future starting to break in right now in our present need.

WATCH

Use these statements to follow along as you watch video session 6.

Three insights to help get the most out of Psalm 100:

1. A spirit of praise to God is a big deal.

2. A spirit of praise to God is healthy, freeing, and uplifting.

3. A spirit of praise to God is not dainty.

To access the teaching sessions,
use the instructions in the back
of your Bible study book.

DISCUSS

Use these questions and prompts to discuss the video teaching.

Has there ever been a time when you were overcome with joyfulness and praise to God? What led to that experience?

Paul instructs us to "rejoice always" in 1 Thessalonians 5:16a. What does that mean? Is it even possible? Has there ever been a time when you struggled to feel any joy at all?

As we've been discovering throughout this study, the Psalms span a wide range of human emotion. And we can relate to them all. God created us to feel deeply. Living on a sin-cursed earth poses a challenge for us there. Pain and struggle tempt us to turn our emotions downward and inward. How can we rejoice always? Why does God's Word even instruct us to rejoice always?

Read Psalm 100 and review the three insights Ray gave to help us make the most out of it.

1. A spirit of praise to God is a big deal.

2. A spirit of praise to God is healthy, freeing, and uplifting.

3. A spirit of praise to God is not dainty.

What are some real-life ways you apply the instruction of Psalm 100:1, "Make a joyful noise to the LORD"? What about ways that extend beyond singing in worship?

Ray explained that a spirit of praise is not trivial or superficial; rather, it is essential. Have you found that true in your own life? How so? If not, what holds you back?

Note again the superscription of Psalm 100 ("A psalm for giving thanks"). How does the concept of scripting and scheduling joyful praise to God strike you? How does this speak to the importance of engaging regularly in corporate worship?

What danger is there in only praising God when you feel like it?

How does understanding the meaning of "make a joyful noise" (v. 1) as a war cry and "gladness" (v. 2) as merriment or mirth make you feel: uncomfortable, liberated, confused, appreciative, resistant, other? Explain.

We have learned much in these six weeks about who God is. What stands out to you most as reasons to joyfully shout with the psalmist, "For the LORD is good; His steadfast love endures forever, and His faithfulness to all generations" (v. 5)?

What remaining questions or comments do you have about this session's teaching video? What was challenging, convicting, encouraging, or timely for your current circumstances?

CLOSE IN PRAYER

Prayer Requests

PSALM 100

OUTLINE FOR PSALM 100

How: make a joyful noise, serve, come (1-2)

Why: He is God, He made us, we are His (3)

How: enter, give thanks, bless (4)

Why: He is good, He is loving, He is faithful (5)

How often do you sing songs of praise and worship to God—regularly throughout the week, only at church on Sundays, or hardly ever?

What are some reasons why a believer might not engage regularly in singing songs of praise? What are some reasons why a believer might prioritize that as regular practice?

Some Christians think singing is an optional extra, or that something else is the better answer to bringing change to the world—like a focus on politics, for example. But a spirit of praise to God, a spirit of rejoicing in God and thanks to God and singing our heads off to God is a really big deal. God has designed reality in such a way that we *praise* our way into a better future (See 2 Chronicles 20:1-23 and Acts 16:16-26, for example). That's not only true in Scripture. Think of it in terms of life today.

What are some of the various ways you seek to enact change in the world (for example, politics, service, invention)? Compared to these, how is singing loud praises to your Lord Jesus Christ impactful?

SING, SERVE, COME

Make a joyful noise to the LORD, all the earth!
Serve the LORD with gladness!
Come into his presence with singing!

PSALM 100:1-2

Making a joyful noise, serving with gladness, and coming into His presence with singing are not "religious" activities. They are the kinds of things we all do when the good guy wins! They're like a standing ovation at the end of an amazing concert or a an exciting sporting event. It is not refined; it is raucous.

> **In what context(s) is it natural for you to celebrate raucously? Why is it often easier for many people to make a joyful noise in other contexts than it is in worship of the Lord? What might that say about us?**

> **Which do you most associate with serving: drudgery, duty, gladness, purpose, or something else? Why?**

The psalmist not only exhorts us to celebrate the Lord loudly; he wants us to serve the Lord with gladness, too. But service, even in the context of the corporate body of Christ, often feels to us more like duty and even drudgery. We think of service as a "have to," not a "get to." God wants to help us flip the script.

> **We tend to think that joy comes before praise. But Psalm 100 indicates that praise leads to joy. How can this truth energize your worship and your service, particularly when you do not feel joyful?**

KNOW THAT HE IS GOD

Know that the LORD, he is God!
It is he who made us, and we are his;
we are his people, and the sheep of his pasture.

PSALM 100:3

In this verse, what reasons does the psalmist give you to praise Jesus?

The act of singing itself is not proof of full and pure trust in Jesus. So how can you know whether your praise is based on head knowledge, temporary emotion, or genuine heartfelt belief?

Jesus came right out and said it: "I am the truth" (John 14:6). And Psalm 100 says He is God. This is reason to praise Him! That He made us and we are His people and the sheep of His pasture is *more* reason to joyfully praise Him. We are not self-made. We do not invent our purpose in life. We are His ongoing miracle, walking in His sovereign purpose. That is true about us as a the body of Christ, and it's true about us as individual people.

We are *His* people and the sheep of *His* pasture. And we know why sheep were brought into the temple: for sacrifice. Here's how crazy our joy is when it is centered on the gospel of Jesus Christ: We're so done with our own self-protection that we feel *freed* when we're living and dying for Him. We *want* our lives to count for Jesus, no matter what that costs.

ENTER HIS GATES

Enter his gates with thanksgiving,
and his courts with praise!
Give thanks to him; bless his name!

PSALM 100:4

Have there been times in your life when you've been more passionate about worship than others? What causes you to feel passionate or apathetic about worshiping Christ?

What does verse 4 imply about how to experience continual joy? What responsibility has God given you besides simply showing up at church?

The psalm invites us further in, more and more deeply and intimately—from the gates, to the courts, to the Lord himself, His very name. When the heart of a Christian starts feeling, "I want Jesus, but I don't want *too much* of Him—not so much that He takes over," it should serve as a warning sign. That's how people, and even whole churches, begin to tank. Jesus knows when He isn't wanted anymore. And the world doesn't need even one more Bible-believing, dead church.

What steps can you take to stay open and eager for more of God's glory in the gospel? What steps should a local church take to stay open and eager for more of God's glory?

HIS LOVE ENDURES FOREVER

For the LORD is good;

his steadfast love endures forever,

and his faithfulness to all generations.

PSALM 100:5

What in verse 5 stands out to you as a reason to keep reaching for joy?

How has God shown *you* His goodness, love, and faithfulness in uncertain times?

At the cross Jesus opened His veins to prove that God is *for you*—He is good and steadfast and faithful for the long haul. Jesus died to prove that God will never get tired of being good to you and loving you and standing by you. It's not a decision God makes on a case-by-case basis, so that you never know which way He's going to go. Goodness, love, and faithfulness are just *who God is* to sinners who come to Him holding out the empty hands of faith. We don't know how events will unfold, but we do know who God is.

Let's never tell ourselves, "When my schedule is less stressful and I have more space in my life, I'll get around to praising God." The fact is, the people happiest about Jesus have always been the ones facing the deepest hardship.

PSALM 100
REAL JOY

Use the spaces below to journal a prayer or response to each prompt.

SIMPLICITY. We all struggle with many sins, and Romans 1:21 traces them all down to this root cause: "Although they knew God, they did not honor him as God *or give thanks to him*" (emphasis added). When we've lost a simple heart of thanks to God, everything starts breaking down. What is a sin that you struggle with? Joy in the Lord will help you overcome it.

VITALITY. A spirit of praise impacts personal health and buoyancy. Praising God is the kale of the soul. Let the layers of frustration and sulking and pouting peel off of you. Let it go, look to the Lord, and your heart will come *alive* again.

ANTICIPATION. A church set apart to God by a spirit of praise will always be prophetic in this world, until Christ returns. Your joy in these times, along with all the saints, foretells of the eternal joy still to come.

CENTER. Nothing is more miserable than self-centered obliviousness. And nothing is more liberating, happy, and compelling than letting go of brooding and personal agendas and praising the Lord that He is God and we are not. If we will humble ourselves and reverently keep the Lord at the center, we will have energy for fighting on.

PSALM 126

OUTLINE FOR PSALM 126
Promises of renewal (1-3)
Prayers for restoration (4-6)

We began our previous study with a question about singing. Let's begin this one with a similar question about praying: How often do you ask God to do great things that only He can do—regularly throughout the week, only when I'm really desperate, or hardly ever?

What are some reasons why a believer might not ask God to do great, far-reaching things that are beyond human ability?

What does it say about someone who expectantly prays for God to do extraordinary things that only He can do?

Prayer is asking God for the great things *only He* can do, and anyone can pray that way. In Psalm 126, we find that sort of expectancy as our example and real joy as its effect.

Who are these praying people in Psalm 126? They are broken people. They are captive people. They are weeping people. They are praying with expectancy not because their circumstances give them any hope, but because they know who they are praying *to*. He is the God who restores, gives laughter, and does great things for weak people. And you can pray this way, too. God will do great things for *you*.

GOD'S PROMISE OF RENEWAL

When the LORD restored the fortunes of Zion,
  we were like those who dream.
Then our mouth was filled with laughter,
  and our tongue with shouts of joy;
then they said among the nations,
  "The LORD has done great things for them."
The LORD has done great things for us;
  we are glad.

PSALM 126:1-3

Would you want anything less than this—to say, "The LORD has done great things for us; we are glad"? When you were a kid and someone asked you what you wanted to be when you grew up, did you say, "When I grow up, I want to be mediocre! I want a life that won't count!"? Not likely! When we're young, we have stars in our eyes.

The same isn't often said of us as we grow older, though. Over time, what causes so many people to settle into mediocrity? Has this happened to you?

As the years go by, some of that youthful passion gets beaten out of us—like these people in Psalm 126. The NASB translation helps us understand why. It puts verse 1 like this: "When the LORD brought back the captives of Zion."

What are some modern-day sources of "captivity" that steal our joy?

Sooner or later we all find ourselves in captivity of some kind. We look around and wonder, "How on earth did I get here? Is this the life I'm stuck with now?" Psalm 126 tells us that God listens for the prayers of *captives*. God wants to set us free and give us our youthful enthusiasm back. That's why Psalm 126 is in the Bible. It is about new beginnings—through prayer.

> **Read Psalm 103:5. How is God always a source of renewal to you? What does it look like to embrace this kind of renewal?**

God's promise of renewal for you is not something you can only dream about but never truly experience. In fact, the word for *dream* in Psalm 126:1 is almost always used for God-given dreams prophesying future events. So we might paraphrase verses 1-3 like this: "When the Lord restores our fortunes, when God heals our brokenness, when God frees us from our captivity, that's when our mouths will be filled with laughter. Right now our eyes are filled with tears. But we know that God has great things in store for us. The whole world is going to look on in wonder. And right now, as we savor God's promises by faith, we are thrilled."

> **In what capacities do you most often look forward to God doing great things for you? Rank the following in order from greatest (1) to least (5):**
>
> ☐ **Finances**
> ☐ **Health**
> ☐ **The gospel**
> ☐ **Relationships (marriage, children, friends, etc.)**
> ☐ **A successful career**

Do not let this world tell you your story. Their version is too small. Don't even define yourself. Let the great things of God define you. Only He can satisfy you. His love for you is not a spare corner in His heart. The love He has put upon you surges out of His inconceivably vast heart. How *great* are the thoughts of God toward you! What a *great* thing God has done for you in your salvation.

OUR RESPONSE TO GOD'S PROMISES

Restore our fortunes, O LORD,
    like streams in the Negeb!
Those who sow in tears
    shall reap with shouts of joy!
He who goes out weeping,
    bearing the seed for sowing,
shall come home with shouts of joy,
    bringing his sheaves with him.

PSALM 126:4-6

Now we know what to do with the promises of God. We turn them into *prayer* and *work*. Verses 5-6 teach us to roll up our sleeves and work and weep. Our very tears are the seed sown for a harvest of new life. And those efforts and tears *will* bring in a joyful harvest. But verse 4 teaches us how to pray, "Restore our fortunes."

This is the gospel story. God gave us everything, we gave Him grief, and then He acted to "restore our fortunes." How did He do that?

God gave us everything back again—and infinitely more in Christ. He took our guilt onto Himself at the cross, to the point of death. But He rose up from it all with new life, and now His kingdom powers are giving ruined people their lives back—anyone who will receive Him. We've only begun to see what He will do. Everything will change by His kingdom power. We will never be the same again. The cure has begun, and He is coming again to destroy all evil and take us home forever.

What does God want from you in the meantime—to pray only for your ultimate restoration in heaven, or to pray even for personal restoration here today? In what situation do you need restoration today?

God wants you to take His promises in the Bible and pray those blessings down. Even if you've bungled your life, this is for you. God's people back then squandered their opportunity. He meant for them to be a blessing to the whole world, but they drove into a ditch. And here in Psalm 126, He coaches them in how to pray their way back.

What does the simile "like streams in the Negeb" say about the level of expectation you should have in praying God's promises for your life today?

The Negeb is the desert, south of Jerusalem. It's a place of drought and barrenness. But there are rain storms in the Negeb that suddenly and surprisingly flood that desert. Verses 5-6 remind us that joyful success comes through our own rugged work. We embrace the dignity of our work together. But verse 4 is a still more wonderful truth. God is able at any time to send a *downpour* of blessing, like torrential streams flooding the desert.

If you desire above all else what *only God* can do, then *pray* for that. Your strongly established idolatries and captivities can be swept away by the sudden outgushing of God's blessing. So why not put away small prayers and low expectations and cry out to Him to restore your joy?

God gave you this prayer in Psalm 126. He likes this prayer, and He is ready to answer it. Is there any reason not to pray for God to restore your fortunes, not only one day in heaven but even now, here on earth? Use this space to write that prayer.

What is one true or key insight you're going to take away from this study?

PSALM 126
REAL JOY

Use the spaces below to journal a prayer or response to each prompt.

GREATNESS. The gospel takes you to the mountaintop of God's promises to see the promised land—out beyond the disappointments, brutalities, and stupidities of the moment. Seeing the great things God will do has the power to lift you above self-pity, refusal to risk, and captivity to fear. And He wants to take you into the gladness of His greatness right now.

BOLDNESS. Do you long for what only God can do? Romans 4:17 says that God calls into existence things that don't even exist yet. He does great things, and when you pray with expectation of His incredible will to be made known, He will answer.

LAUGHTER. What the gospel reveals is a future that will fill your mouth with laughter. The gospel has a forward tilt to it, because hope for the future is what keeps you alive right now. With a great future breathing great life into you today, you can face *anything*.

RICHES. Everything you desire is in Christ's treasure—pleasures forevermore, rivers of delight, fullness of joy, and infinitely more. His immense riches are yours forever through the finished work of Christ on the cross. But you must choose. Your dream can be filled with the best things this world has to offer. But if your heart longs for more, Jesus Christ offers you great things—freely through His grace. Will you say, "Lord, I choose you today"?

PSALMS OF SHARED PRAISE

To recap some of what we have learned in these weeks of *Psalms: Real Help for Real Life*, the Psalms give us gospel insight, pointing us forward to Jesus and His amazing grace. Sin gives us reason to lament; Jesus's redemption of us in our sin gives us reason to rejoice in continual praise. Yet we struggle, with both lament and praise. And one impacts the other. When we understand the depth of our need for Christ, our expressions of joy in Christ will necessarily become less refined and reserved, and we will join together in raucous praise.

As a way of stepping into a spirit of continual praise and rejoicing, consider how you might put into practice the study helps Ray gave in this week's Going Deeper teaching.

Record the burst of praise that concludes each section of Psalms. Then repeat those aloud to the Lord in the exclamatory spirit with which they were written.

Book 1, Psalm 1-41 (Psalm 41:13):

Book 2, Psalm 42-72 (Psalm 72:19):

Book 3, Psalm 73-89 (Psalm 89:52):

Book 4, Psalm 90-106 (Psalm 106:48):

Book 5, Psalm 107-150 (Psalm 146:1; 147:1; 148:1; 149:1; 150:1-6):

Psalm 33:1 declares, "Praise befits the upright." How is the Lord speaking to you about what a spirit of praise does in a church?

What is your role in that? Would you categorize your praise to the Lord as limited or unlimited? Why?

What needs to change in your life so that you give the Lord everything you have in praise to Him going forward? How can your continued study of the Psalms help you in that?

To access the teaching sessions, use the instructions in the back of your Bible study book.

LEADER

GUIDE

TIPS FOR LEADING A SMALL GROUP

Follow these guidelines to prepare for each session.

PRAYERFULLY PREPARE

REVIEW. Review the personal studies and group questions ahead of time.

PRAY. Be intentional about praying for each person in the group. Ask the Holy Spirit to work through you and the group discussion as you point to Jesus each week through God's Word.

MINIMIZE DISTRACTIONS

Create a comfortable environment. If group members are uncomfortable, they'll be distracted and therefore not engaged in the group experience. Plan ahead by considering these details:

seating	food or drink
temperature	surrounding noise
lighting	general cleanliness

At best, thoughtfulness and hospitality show guests and group members they're welcome and valued in whatever environment you choose to gather. At worst, people may never notice your effort, but they're also not distracted. Do everything in your ability to help people focus on what's most important: connecting with God, with the Bible, and with one another.

INCLUDE OTHERS

Your goal is to foster a community in which people are welcome just as they are but encouraged to grow spiritually. Always be aware of opportunities to include any people who visit the group and to invite new people to join your group. An inexpensive way to make first-time guests feel welcome or to invite someone to get involved is to give them their own copies of this Bible study book.

ENCOURAGE DISCUSSION

A good small group experience has the following characteristics:

EVERYONE PARTICIPATES. Encourage everyone to ask questions, share responses, or read aloud.

NO ONE DOMINATES—NOT EVEN THE LEADER. Be sure that your time speaking as a leader takes up less than half of your time together as a group. Politely guide discussion if anyone dominates.

NOBODY IS RUSHED THROUGH QUESTIONS. Don't feel that a moment of silence is a bad thing. People often need time to think about their responses or to gain courage to share what God is stirring in their hearts.

INPUT IS AFFIRMED AND FOLLOWED UP. Make sure you point out something true or helpful in a response. Don't just move on. Build community with follow-up questions, asking how other people have experienced similar things or how a truth has shaped their understanding of God and the Scripture you're studying. People are less likely to speak up if they fear that you don't actually want to hear their answers or that you're looking for only a certain answer.

GOD AND HIS WORD ARE CENTRAL. Opinions and experiences can be helpful, but God has given us the truth. Trust God's Word to be the authority and God's Spirit to work in people's lives. You can't change anyone, but God can. Continually point people to the Word and to active steps of faith.

KEEP CONNECTING

Think of ways to connect with group members during the week. Participation during the group session is always improved when members spend time connecting with one another outside the group sessions. The more people are comfortable with and involved in one another's lives, the more they'll look forward to being together. When people move beyond being friendly to truly being friends who form a community, they come to each session eager to engage instead of merely attending.

When possible, build deeper friendships by planning or spontaneously inviting group members to join you outside your regularly scheduled group time for activities, meals, group hangouts, or projects around your home, church, or community.

PSALMS LEADER GUIDE

SESSION ONE

KEY SCRIPTURE

Psalms 1 and 2

SESSION OUTLINE

1. These two psalms introduce the whole book.
2. Psalm 1 is marked with strong contrasts, with wise personal guidance.
3. Psalm 2 is equally bold, with hope for the entire world.

BEFORE THE SESSION

1. Review the group content as well as the video teaching session.
2. Read and review Psalms 1–2, making your own observations about the Scriptures.
3. Decide whether you're going to watch the video teaching sessions together or if you want group members to watch them prior to the group meeting. Each video is around ten to fifteen minutes long.
4. Pray for all group members by name.
5. Review the questions in the Start and Discuss sections. Feel free to adjust or adapt the questions provided to better fit the members of your group.

DURING THE SESSION

1. Make sure everyone is acquainted with one another. Consider sharing names and brief information so everyone feels welcomed and included.
2. Focus the attention of the group by pointing out that the Psalms offer real help for real life. Ask if there is a particular area of life where they feel like they need the help the Psalms offer.
3. If people are unfamiliar with the Psalms as a book or a genre, explain Psalms is a book of sacred songs—songs of praise and songs of lament. It was written to direct the worship of God's people.

4. Help them to see that God's Word is a place that we can go for help and comfort because we meet the living Christ through the Psalms.
5. Be sensitive towards those for whom this is their first Bible study experience.
6. Encourage them to begin a journey through the Psalms on their own using this book as a guide. State that we will be given many helps for understanding the Psalms as we progress through the study.
7. Close in prayer.
8. Remind them to complete the two Personal Studies and the Going Deeper section before the next meeting.

AFTER THE SESSION

Consider meeting in groups of two or three to discuss and review the guided reading. Here are a few questions to ask during that time. Alternately, you might consider sending these questions to the group in a text or email to consider on their own.

Which of the words on page 19 did you find most helpful? Why?

What is the most significant takeaway from the first week of study?

What is one way this week's Going Deeper section about reading and interpreting Psalms helps you become a better reader of the Psalms?

NOTES

PSALMS LEADER GUIDE

SESSION TWO

KEY SCRIPTURE

Psalms 23 and 130

SESSION OUTLINE

Consider three aspects in Psalm 23:
1. The personal nature of the psalm.
2. The trajectory of the psalm.
3. The spirit of the psalm.

BEFORE THE SESSION

1. Review the group content as well as the video teaching session.
2. Read and review Psalm 23, making your own observations about the Scripture. Use last week's Going Deeper section to help you get the most of this psalm.
3. Watch the group teaching video prior to the session.
4. Pray for all group members by name.
5. Review the questions in the Start and Discuss sections. Feel free to adjust or adapt the questions provided to better fit the members of your group.

DURING THE SESSION

1. Welcome any new guests.
2. Begin by looking back at the previous week. Ask what questions there were. Invite members to share insights or things that the Lord is doing in their life through the Psalms.
3. Note that this week we will be covering Psalm 23, which is one of the most well-known pieces of Scripture. Many with no faith background are familiar with it.

4. Rest can be hard to come by these days. Invite people to share where they are looking for God's rest. Expect that this might take many a few minutes to answer.

5. Even thought this is a well-loved psalm, resist the urge to make assumptions about it. Allow yourself and the group to experience God's Word afresh through this reading and group time.

6. Highlight that we all experience crisis in life and that David found himself in a moment of crisis writing this psalm. Acknowledge that the crisis is real, but it is less important and less real than the God who was with David.

7. Assure them that the God who was with David is with them too.

8. Close in prayer.

9. Remind them to complete the two Personal Studies and the Going Deeper section before the next meeting.

AFTER THE SESSION

Consider meeting in groups of two or three to discuss and review the guided reading. Here are a few questions to ask during that time. Alternately, you might consider sending these questions to the group in a text or email to consider on their own.

One of the key truths of this session is that for those of us in Christ, you are not the only one working for you. In light of that, consider again, what situation tempts you to think, speak, or act as if all you have going for you is you? How does Psalm 23 encourage you in that situation?

Psalm 23 uses many personal pronouns. What does taking notice of their frequency help us understand about God and His nature?

NOTES

PSALMS LEADER GUIDE

SESSION THREE

KEY SCRIPTURE

Psalms 51 and 73

SESSION OUTLINE

1. The backstory
2. The climax
3. The conclusion

BEFORE THE SESSION

1. Review the group content as well as the video teaching session.
2. Read and review Psalm 51, making your own observations about the Scripture.
3. Consider a time when you've been in a similar situation as David in Psalm 51.
4. Watch the group teaching video prior to the session.
5. Pray for all group members by name.
6. Review the questions in the Start and Discuss sections. Feel free to adjust or adapt the questions provided to better fit the members of your group.

DURING THE SESSION

1. Begin by looking back at the previous week. Ask what questions there were. Invite members to share insights or things that the Lord is doing in their life through the Psalms.
2. Make sure to cover the backstory of Psalm 51. If time allows, read through 2 Samuel 11–12 together.
3. Take note that repentance is a necessary part of the Christian life. Psalm 51 gives us permission to be honest with God. God is able to take the full weight of our honesty.

4. Remind the group that when we're caught in a sinful pattern it may seem tempting or desirable to hide our sin. However, we cannot hid our sin from God and holding on to sin instead of confessing it honestly is corrosive to our souls and relationships.

5. Close in prayer.

6. Remind them to complete the two Personal Studies and the Going Deeper section before the next meeting.

AFTER THE SESSION

Consider meeting in groups of two or three to discuss and review the guided reading. Here are a few questions to ask during that time. Alternately, you might consider sending these questions to the group in a text or email to consider on their own.

In what current situation do you need God's help of real honesty? Take this moment as a nudge to get honest with God.

Real faith asks hard questions. What questions do you have? What might God, through the Scriptures, have to say about those questions?

Why is confession of sins a necessary part of real faith in Jesus?

NOTES

PSALMS LEADER GUIDE

SESSION FOUR

KEY SCRIPTURE

Psalms 85 and 42/43

SESSION OUTLINE

1. The structure
2. Words of wrath
3. Key words

BEFORE THE SESSION

1. Review the group content as well as the video teaching session.
2. Read and review Psalm 85, making your own observations about the Scripture.
3. Pray through your own hope. Find the place where you need hope in the Lord.
4. Watch the group teaching video prior to the session.
5. Pray for all group members by name.
6. Review the questions in the Start and Discuss sections. Feel free to adjust or adapt the questions provided to better fit the members of your group.

DURING THE SESSION

1. Begin by looking back at the previous week. Ask what questions there were. Invite members to share insights or things that the Lord is doing in their life through the Psalms.
2. Highlight the main point that God loves to give His best to people who deserve His worst. That is the cornerstone of our hope—that we are loved beyond anything we could ever imagine.
3. Be sure to hit that Psalm 85 doesn't minimize or ignore our sin or our need. Rather, it is honest about the divide between who God is and who we are.

4. Double down on the key words that Ray highlighted, such as: *revive* (v. 6), *again* (vv. 4,6), *steadfast love and faithfulness* (v. 10), *folly* (v. 8), and *fear* (v. 9).

5. Hope is a felt need that many people are acutely aware of. Be prepared to instill hope and point people to the gospel.

6. Close in prayer.

7. Remind them to complete the two Personal Studies and the Going Deeper section before the next meeting.

AFTER THE SESSION

Consider meeting in groups of two or three to discuss and review the guided reading. Here are a few questions to ask during that time. Alternately, you might consider sending these questions to the group in a text or email to consider on their own.

Which of the key words in Psalm 85, or what other word in Psalm 85, opens up the whole psalm for you most personally? In what way?

Take a look at the key words on page 79. Which one is most resonant with you?

The Going Deeper video this week was about the Psalms as a daily resource. This week you're more than halfway through with this study. What benefits could you see in using the Psalms daily?

NOTES

PSALMS LEADER GUIDE

SESSION FIVE

KEY SCRIPTURE

Psalms 139 and 27

SESSION OUTLINE

Consider three aspects in Psalm 139:

1. Hatred in verses 21-22—"I hate them with complete hatred."
2. Pivot in verse 18—"I am awake, and I am still with you."
3. Courage throughout verses 1-24—"You have searched me and known me. . . . Where shall I flee from your presence? . . . You knitted me together in my mother's womb. . . . Lead me in the way everlasting!"

BEFORE THE SESSION

1. Review the group content as well as the video teaching session.
2. Read and review Psalm 139, making your own observations about the Scripture.
3. Consider a time when you've needed courage from the Lord.
4. Watch the group teaching video prior to the session.
5. If this group will continue to meet beyond this study, communicate what is next.
6. Pray for all group members by name.
7. Review the questions in the Start and Discuss sections. Feel free to adjust or adapt the questions provided to better fit the members of your group.

DURING THE SESSION

1. Begin by looking back at the previous week. Ask what questions there were. Invite members to share insights or things that the Lord is doing in their life through the Psalms.
2. Work through Psalm 139 together with Ray's outline.

3. Note that although Psalm 139 is frequently used (for good reason) in talks about life and human dignity, it is possible that many of us have read Psalm 139 numerous times without realizing that David's context was personal suffering at the hands of evil adversaries.

4. Since that is the case, many of us have a lot in common with David. Our adversaries may not be as imposing as David's, but we all have situations where we need to cultivate and exert courage.

5. Close in prayer.

6. Remind them to complete the two Personal Studies and the Going Deeper section before the next meeting.

7. Announce to the group what you will be studying after the conclusion of this study in Psalms.

AFTER THE SESSION

Consider meeting in groups of two or three to discuss and review the guided reading. Here are a few questions to ask during that time. Alternately, you might consider sending these questions to the group in a text or email to consider on their own.

What would it look like for us to live courageously in Christ this week?

Read Psalm 139:1-6. Some think it is a fearful thing to be searched and known by God. What about you? How do you feel knowing that God completely knows your activity, thoughts, path, words, and intentions?

What did you think about this week's Going Deeper? Why is it essential to read the Psalms for gospel insight?

NOTES

PSALMS LEADER GUIDE

SESSION SIX

KEY SCRIPTURE

Psalms 100 and 126

SESSION OUTLINE

1. A spirit of praise to God is a big deal.
2. A spirit of praise to God is healthy, freeing, and uplifting.
3. A spirit of praise to God is not dainty.

BEFORE THE SESSION

1. Review the group content as well as the video teaching session.
2. Read and review Psalm 100 making your own observations about the Scripture.
3. Watch the group teaching video prior to the session.
4. Pray for all group members by name.
5. Review the questions in the Start and Discuss sections. Feel free to adjust or adapt the questions provided to better fit the members of your group.
6. Make plans for what you're doing with the groups after this study has concluded.

DURING THE SESSION

1. Invite members to share key takeaways from your time together in this study.
2. Define praise for the group. Help them to see that it is more than worshiping through song, though it certainly includes musical worship.
3. Point out that this is the culmination of our study for a reason. A spirit of joy flows from everything else we've learned about God and ourselves through the Psalms.

4. Note that is it possible to be joyful despite your circumstances. When joy is attached to Christ it transcends anything that happens to us. This doesn't mean that we will never experience pain or struggle, but that Christ is with us through them and our joy is secure in Him.
5. Close in prayer.
6. If this is an ongoing group, make sure everyone knows what you're studying after Psalms and has what they need for that study.

AFTER THE SESSION

Consider meeting in groups of two or three to discuss and review the guided reading. Here are a few questions to ask during that time. Alternately, you might consider sending these questions to the group in a text or email to consider on their own.

How will you interact with the Psalms differently as a result of this study?

What danger is there in only praising God when you feel like it?

What remaining questions or comments do you have about this study? What was challenging, convicting, encouraging, or timely for your current circumstances?

NOTES

If only Solomon had written a book on wisdom.

Oh, wait.

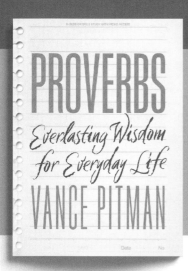

Take a month-long journey through all 31 chapters of Proverbs. You'll not only gain an appreciation for this popular and applicable book of the Bible, you'll also begin to develop a daily habit of seeking wisdom from God's Word. In addition to the four session videos, you get access to 31 short, daily teaching videos (one for each chapter), all included in the purchase price of the *Bible Study Book*.

Get real help for real life.

Through the Psalms, God is inviting you to a deeper place with Him where you can find help, rest, honesty, hope, courage, and joy.

In this study you'll:

- Learn to be a better reader of Psalms.
- Find hope in your current struggles.
- Be restored into a deep and abiding relationship with God.
- Take your hurt to God and be received as a beloved son or daughter.

STUDYING ON YOUR OWN?

Be sure to watch Ray Ortlund's video teaching sessions, available through the redemption code printed in this *Bible Study Book*.

LEADING A GROUP?

Each group member will need a *Psalms Bible Study Book*, which includes video access. Because all participants will have access to the video content, you can choose to watch the videos outside of your group meeting if desired. Or, if you're watching together and someone misses a group meeting, they'll have the flexibility to catch up! A DVD set is also available to purchase separately if desired.

ADDITIONAL RESOURCES

BIBLE STUDY eBOOK WITH VIDEO ACCESS

The eBook includes the content of this printed book but offers the convenience and flexibility that comes with mobile technology.

005840906 **$19.99**

DVD SET

This option is for anyone who has unreliable internet service or simply wants a physical copy of the videos.

005840917 **$29.99**

Browse study formats, a free session sample, video clips, church promotional materials, and more at lifeway.com/psalms.